Fire to the Earth

The Heart of the Saints

FR KEN BARKER MGL

Modotti Press

Published in 2017 by Modotti Press, an imprint of Connor Court Publishing Pty Ltd

Copyright © Fr Ken Barker MGL

All rights reserved. No part of this book may be reproduced or transmitted in any form or by any means, electronic or mechanical, including photocopying, recording or by any information storage and retrieval system, without prior permission in writing from the publisher.

Connor Court Publishing Pty Ltd
PO Box 7257
Redland Bay QLD 4165, Australia
sales@connorcourt.com
www.connorcourt.com
Phone 0497-900-685

ISBN: 978-1-925501-54-4

Nihil Obstat
Rev Warrick Tonkin BA, Dip Ed, Bth, BTheol, M.Ed
Censor Deputatis

Imprimatur
Most Rev Christopher Prowse DD STD
Archbishop of Canberra and Goulburn

Front Cover Design: Lawrence Yuen MGL

Bible quotations are from the New Revised Standard Version Bible, copyright 1989, Division of Christian Education of the National Council of the Churches of Christ in the United States of America. Used by permission. All rights reserved.

I want to especially express my gratitude to Selina Hasham for working on the text in preparation for publication and also for writing the inspiring Introduction. A hearty thanks to Lawrence Yuen MGL who designed such a beautiful cover. And I am grateful to my MGL brothers for their patience with me, and for all their support and encouragement. I am dedicating this book to the ten saints who are presented here, praying that they will continue to intercede for us.

TABLE OF CONTENTS

FOREWORD	5
INTRODUCTION	9
FRANCIS OF ASSISI	13
CLARE OF ASSISI	35
DOMINIC GUZMAN	49
CATHERINE OF SIENA	69
IGNATIUS LOYOLA	91
TERESA OF AVILA	119
FRANCIS DE SALES	139
MARGARET MARY ALOCOQUE	159
ALPHONSUS LIGUORI	175
THERESE OF LISIEUX	195
THE HEART OF THE SAINTS:	
The Light of God's Love	209
Endnotes	219

FOREWORD

In the year 2000 I remember sitting in a crowd of 2 million young people at the Jubilee World Youth Day in Rome. I was sharing an ear phone with another pilgrim as we listened to an address of Pope John Paul II translated into English across a crackling frequency.

For a young person it was a daunting time. With much anticipation and not without trepidation the 21st century had just ticked over. Our computers didn't crash but plenty was still unknown as we balanced on the cusp between two millennia, wondering what the future would hold.

Leaning in to try and hear properly I remember being stuck by what the Pope said. Into all of my uncertainty, the Holy Father's words cut deeply, "Young people of every continent, do not be afraid to be the saints of the new millennium!"

Us? Ordinary young people? Saints?

Is that even possible?

The saints I knew at that time were untouchable and perfect. The gap between them and I was great. However, John Paul II brought holiness and sainthood within reach for all people, in every circumstance of life and at any age.

In this book Fr Ken profiles men and women who, though imperfect, ended up living lives of extraordinary heroism, courage and love. As I read these pages I came to know these saints as ordinary and likeable people.

We should be wary of enshrining these figures in the hagiographic display cabinet of history. They would be the first to protest. They did not live exemplary lives to be remembered as pious figures of the past. They poured out their lives for Jesus so that the Church could continue its mission of setting the earth ablaze with the fire of God's love. In their time and throughout the ages their faith gives life and relevance to the Church from the thirteenth century until today. I believe their sacrifices are enhanced by the contributions of the holy people of our time, continuing the Gospel story of which we all play our part.

This is not a history book. Through the lens of eternity these saints are living persons who intercede for us today. The Church in her wisdom has called them saints and Fr Ken's unique perspective on each of them helps us see why. Let him take you on a journey of getting to know them, and while on that journey, listen to the voice of the Spirit that might be speaking to you through their stories. We can look forward to meeting these charming and indomitable characters in heaven and I thank Fr Ken for making that meeting a more familiar and happy one.

Reading these accounts, it was remarkable to me the reliance the saints placed on those who went before. Alphonsus Liguori drew on the teachings of Francis de Sales. Francis de Sales was inspired by the spirituality of Teresa of Avila. Sainthood is contagious! If we make a choice to live holy lives, we just might start a chain reaction that never ends.

Though I might not be living in the charming hills of Assisi or the medieval town of Avila, the urban metropolis of Sydney is the landscape in which I am challenged to live a holy life, and to give witness to Jesus in my time.

These saints did not live in the third millennium, and yet they are saints for our time. Centuries and millennia change the cultural context in which we live but they do not change the human heart. The saints in this book did not use the internet or own a smart phone, but they understood what it means to be loved and rejected. They were familiar with powerful desires and the temptation to sin. They experienced the hunger to belong and the aspiration to achieve something meaningful in life. They tasted success and failure, and they knew what it feels like to have dreams and regrets. They were just like us.

Fr Ken has devoted his life to calling forth modern day saints in ordinary young Australians, men and women who, despite their ordinariness aren't afraid to say their generous 'yes' to God. As a man of the Church he knows what the Church needs in order to thrive. It doesn't need complex new programs and elaborate strategies of reform. It just needs you and me to be saints.

In my lifetime I have met modern day saints. I hope to meet many more. May you read these pages and hear the gentle call of a loving God to give your life to Him completely.

Selina Hasham

Communications Director

Catholic Archdiocese of Sydney

INTRODUCTION

When we look to the saints we are not trying to slavishly imitate all that they did. Their response to the Lord and their radical way of living the gospel was to meet the challenges of their own time. Our contemporary challenges are different. The saints inspire us to be able to respond to the distinctive call that God has upon our lives in this age. They are shining examples of personal holiness and commitment to the Church's mission of evangelisation. In reading the lives of the saints we need to move from admiration to inspiration; not only to applaud their faithfulness to God's calling on their lives, but also be motivated to make a similar response in our own day in our own circumstances. The call to holiness is for all.

A question may rise in our hearts: are the saints of previous centuries relevant to the realities of daily life in the twenty first century? In opening up the lives and teaching of ten saints in this book I hope to show they are relevant, and that holiness is attainable for any of us. I trust that each saint described in this book will evoke some aspect of the call of the gospel in you, enrich your spiritual journey, and enliven your heart in response to the Lord. When we look closely at the lives of the saints we find that their personal struggles to pray, to live as a disciple, and to go forth on mission, are much the same as ours.

Their cultural context is so different that often it can seem almost alien. But they were human beings like us, suffering from the same anxieties and tensions, the same consolations and desolations, the same triumphs and failures. The crises of faith, the temptations to discouragement, the call to love the unlovable, are all the same. In the spiritual journey we can identify with their aspirations and desire to be holy. We share with them the burden of our broken humanity which seems to be such an impossible obstacle to growth. We can feel and empathise with them as they passionately seek the Lord, but are then tempted to disillusionment, as they are plunged unexpectedly into the darkness of faith. We can feel our hearts stirring with zeal for the kingdom as we read of their apostolic fervour and heroic risks of faith in preaching the gospel. But we can also identify with their frustration in the face of opposition, and long for the grace given to them to stand joyfully when persecuted for their faith.

The saints I have chosen are all religious or priests, with the exception of Catherine of Siena who was a third order Dominican. I encourage the reader, whether lay or religious, to glean from these holy men and women what speaks to your heart. And surely, if you are open to the Spirit, something of the lives of these saints and their teaching will resonate within you.

Having said this I have to admit that my choice of saints was governed by the charism of the Missionaries of God's Love (MGL), a new religious congregation of priests and brothers, and our community of sisters who are well on the road to becoming a religious congregation under the same charism. The male saints presented here have been most influential in the beginnings of the congregation, and the female saints came along as the sisters developed their foundation. These days we tend to embrace them all. After all we can't get enough heavenly patrons to intercede for us. So they are the "Top Ten" saints of the MGL!

Just in case you are about to abandon this book since it seems to be MGL specific, I want to encourage you to stay with it. Maybe flip through and pick out the saint that is most attractive. But if you keep going you may find that each of them will speak something to your heart. I have presented them in chronological order, starting with Francis of Assisi in the early 13th century and ending with Therese of Lisieux at the end of the 19th century. They are all Europeans, which may be a deterrent to some who would want a more widely international mix, but the simple reason is that our spirituality has been fed from this rich European tradition. They are Italian, Spanish or French. The perceptive reader will note threads of spiritual wisdom woven through the teaching of these saints that connect them together and make a united spiritual vision possible. In a general sense we are all called by our baptism to be "missionaries of God's love". My contention is that these saints in various ways contribute towards a baptismal vision which we can all embrace.

I certainly want to show how the lives of these saints inspire us in our way of holiness and evangelisation. But my primary focus is actually on their spiritual teaching which has perennial usefulness. The biographical details for each saint are necessarily sketchy so that more space can be given to their spiritual wisdom. I am assuming that the reader desires to grow in the spiritual life and is looking for helpful teaching to facilitate this growth. I suggest to the reader that you ponder each saint's teaching and ask the question: What relevance has this for me or for my community? From my initial contact with people who have read these pages I have been amazed and edified at the way ordinary Catholics in the pews have been able to tussle with the material and draw from it some "chestnuts" for living the way of Jesus. The emphasis is, as you can imagine, on the love of God. I do not apologise for this since I am deeply convinced that more than anything in the Church today we need to experience the truth of God's love and mercy. This was underlined by Pope Benedict's magnificent first encyclical *Deus Caritas Est, (God is Love)*. And it has been even further promoted by Pope Francis' recent Year of Mercy which was so phenomenally popular in the Church across the world.

We are still "love poor", and so many practising Catholics are yet to experience the in- breaking love of God such that the heart is enlarged and Jesus becomes personally real and dynamically present in their lives. So much of Church life can be caught up in bureaucracy, administration, and procedural demands that the love of God can be lost. We can be so dutifully intent upon the pristine purity of doctrine, and the legalistic demands of moral injunctions, and the strict observance of ritual that we miss the heart of it all. These saints call us to the heart of Jesus broken open in love for the world, and invite us to discover him for the first time, or to rediscover him, as our "first love". They also challenge us to go beyond the peripheries of the Church and reach out to those who are languishing in unfortunately oppressive situations, or have more or less given up on life, since it doesn't make much sense to them anymore. With the heart of Jesus we are to search out the lost, alienated and abandoned and help them find a way home to mother Church.

FRANCIS OF ASSISI

Chronology

1181 - born in Assisi

1205 - call from San Damiano cross

1208 - call of the gospel at the Portiuncla; mission begins

1209 - approval of Pope Innocent III

1219 - visit with the sultan

1224 - receives stigmata on Mt LaVerna

1226 - dies on Oct. 3 at Portiuncla, Assisi.

Quotes

    Lord, make me an instrument of thy peace.
    Where there is hatred, let me sow love,
    Where there is injury, pardon;
    Where there is doubt, faith;
    Where there is despair, hope;
    Where there is darkness, light;
    And where there is sadness, joy.

    O Divine Master, grant that I may not so much seek
    to be consoled as to console,
    to be understood as to understand,
    to be loved, as to love.

    For it is in giving that we receive,
    It is in pardoning that we are pardoned,
    and it is in dying that we are born to eternal life.

        (Prayer attributed to Francis)

We adore you, O Christ, and we bless you because by your holy Cross you have redeemed the world.

When God gave me some friars, there was no one to tell me what I should do; but the Most High himself made it clear to me that I must live the life of the gospel.

FRANCIS OF ASSISI

When the fire of God's love enflames the heart we can't help but change. Love has its own persuasion. The conversion of Francis of Assisi dramatically illustrates this reality. As a young man he rushed headlong into a life of pleasure-seeking and revelling with his friends. He worked in his father's clothing shop, but spent most of his spare time roaming the streets of Assisi with his well-to-do friends, singing love songs, serenading beneath the balconies of local beauties, enjoying well-wined banquets, and celebrating in a high-spirited way. Without purpose in life he was drifting aimlessly, carried along by the next social outing, but with a gnawing emptiness in the heart. He was hungry for love, but it eluded him. Yet, even at this time in his journey there was a natural goodness in him. Once when he was busy at the counter of his father's shop a beggar approached him for money, asking alms for the love of God. He automatically refused the man and ordered him to leave the shop. Then he was hit with a deep feeling of remorse for his unkindness. He ran after the man, begged his forgiveness and gave him a generous donation. He resolved at that moment never to refuse a request made in the name of God.

The change that God was bringing about in Francis' young heart happened over time. All his biographers point to the episode when he experienced being taken captive in battle and imprisoned. He had bravely taken up arms to enlist in a local war between Assisi and the neighbouring town, Perugia. But to his dismay he was taken prisoner. Reports are that during this year of incarceration, true to form, he was full of light-heartedness and always had a cheery word for his fellow prisoners. But he had fragile health. He soon fell seriously ill with some mysterious disease. His jailers decided to set him free and get a ransom price for his release. Having endured the humiliation of imprisonment, and this debilitating disease, he returned to Assisi a chastened man. Still suffering this malady that had laid him low, he was now more open to spiritual things. Having experienced his personal brokenness he was led to realise more his dependency on God.

Where are you going?

Once recovered from his sickness Francis was still eagerly filled with the dream of becoming a noble knight in battle. This was the age of nobility attained by military glory and chivalry. Around this time the Papal armies were engaged in battle in Puglia in the south of Italy. Prince Gentile, a count of Assisi, was leaving to join them, and Francis, keen to be dubbed a knight, decided to offer himself. After spending a small fortune on his equipment he set out full of excitement for the adventure ahead. But when they stopped at Spoleto on the first night, Francis had a dream. A mysterious voice spoke to him, "Francis, where are you going?" He answered that he was going to fight in Puglia. The voice said to him, "Tell me, from whom can you expect the most, the master or the servant?" Francis answered, "The master". The voice then asked, "Why would you follow the servant instead of the master on whom he depends?" Francis knew he was being told to return to Assisi and wait upon what he was meant to do.[1] All were amazed when he returned so soon after having left with such pomp and ceremony a couple of days beforehand. But now he was a changed man. The sickness had allowed him to experience his human fragility, opening him to hear what God was saying, and the voice at Spoleto had spoken deeply to his heart.

Back in Assisi he naturally picked up with his pleasure-seeking friends again, but somehow his heart was no longer in it. He wanted to seek out places of solitude to pray. His friends saw him as "king of the youth" and had even given him a home-made sceptre to symbolise his position among them as the craziest one of all. But they were soon to find out that Francis had been captured by a different foolishness, the madness of a man in love with God. One night as they spilled out into the streets of the sleeping town with all their noisy chants and songs, Francis was no longer at the head of the band, but lagging way behind. A grace had come upon him, a light from God, which gave him clarity about the beauty of God, and how earthly pleasures are empty without him. "Suddenly, he was inundated with such a torrent of love, submerged in such sweetness, that he stood there motionless, neither seeing nor hearing anything. They might have cut him to pieces, he said later, and he would not have moved."[2]

His friends came back looking for him. When they saw him it was obvious to all that something had happened. His whole countenance had changed. Naturally they figured he had fallen in love, and wanted to know who this beautiful woman was. "Francis", they asked, "what is going on in your mind? How come you did not follow us? Are you perhaps daydreaming about getting married?" Francis, reluctantly returning from his interior encounter with God, became aware of their presence and answered wistfully, "Yes, it is true. I was dreaming of taking as my wife a young woman who is nobler, wealthier and more beautiful than any of you have ever seen before". Still coming to understand fully what was happening to him, Francis knew he had fallen in love with God, and that this experience of the fire of God's love had won his heart. Commentators have often identified this beautiful woman as "Lady Poverty". That may well be so. But there is no doubt that the turning point in the heart of Francis towards a new way of life was not primarily falling in love with poverty itself, but rather falling in love with Jesus, the poor one, who is to be found in the poor.

San Damiano

Having experienced the fire of God's love poured into his heart by the Holy Spirit, Francis was drawn more and more to secluded places to be alone with the Lord. One of these was a little dilapidated Church of San Damiano just outside the walls of Assisi where there was hanging a large, heavy wooden cross with a Byzantine image of Christ painted on it. On his knees before this cross he was accustomed to pray: "Most high and glorious God, bring light to the darkness of my heart. Give me right faith, certain hope, and perfect charity, with deep humility. Give me wisdom and understanding so I might know your holy and true will. Amen".

One day as he was praying before the cross, a voice spoke to him, "Francis, my church lies in ruins. Go rebuild my church". We are told, "These words filled him with the greatest joy and inner light because in spirit he knew that it was indeed Jesus Christ who had spoken to him".[3] Ready to obey immediately, Francis interpreted the words to mean he was to restore the church building which was desperately in need of repair. He must take action. Where to find the resources to do the work? He raced home and took bales of his father's cloth, and anything else he could find, made his way to Foligno and sold it all. Now with a bag full of money he returned to the priest in charge of the church and offered him the cash for restoration. The old priest, unsure of his grounds with Francis' family, refused to take it. But he did allow Francis to stay with him, the money being thrown into a corner of a window by Francis who thought no more about it. Only later was Francis to realise the full implications of these words spoken to him from the cross. His destiny was not only to rebuild some ruined chapels, but to be an instrument for the restoration of the Church itself.

Meanwhile Francis' father, Peter Bernadone, was enraged when he heard what had happened. He seized his son and threw him into the family dungeon in chains. However, when his father left the house for a business trip Francis' mother took pity on him and released him. But his father was intent on redressing the humiliation brought on the family by his recalcitrant son. He brought him before the bishop in a public ecclesiastical court, probably in the piazza of Santa Maria Maggiore, in front of the bishop's palace. In the presence of the assembled townsfolk, after hearing Peter Bernadone's lament, the bishop ordered Francis to restore to his father everything he had taken. Francis replied that he would do so gladly. Then he went into the palace and returned practically naked, carrying his clothes. He said, "Listen, all of you, and mark my words. Hitherto, I have called Peter Bernadone my father; but because I am resolved to serve God I return to him the money on account of which he was so perturbed, and also the clothes I wore which are his; and from now on I will say 'Our Father in heaven', and not 'my father Peter Bernadone'".[4] We can be sure that these words were not spoken coldly and dispassionately. Rather Francis would have been weeping as he spoke them. The bishop for modesty sake, and no doubt touched by the drama unfolding before him, threw his cloak around the young man, while Peter Bernadone disappeared.

Encounter with the Leper

There was another event that was critical in the conversion of Francis; his encounter with a leper. In fact, in Francis' final testament before dying he identifies this meeting as what inspired his conversion: "This is how God inspired me, Brother Francis, to embark upon a life of penance. When I was in sin, the sight of lepers nauseated me beyond measure; but then God himself led me into their company, and I had pity on them. When I had once become acquainted with them, what had previously nauseated me became a source of spiritual and physical consolation for me. After that I did not wait long before leaving the world".⁵

This is how it happened. Francis was riding his horse in the area around Assisi. To his great consternation he noticed a leper approaching him. He felt repugnance and shrunk back drawing the reins up to turn the horse around and ride quickly away. Lepers terrified him. It was commonly thought that any contact would incur disease. Consequently, lepers were limited to colonies by themselves outside of the towns and were not allowed near residential areas. But Francis at this moment of encounter was given a grace from on high. Instead of following the instinct to panic and turn away, he did the exact opposite. He felt a sweetness within his heart inspired by the Holy Spirit uniting him with the heart of Jesus. Dismounting, and shuddering with a mixture of apprehension and exhilaration at the sweet choice he was making, he reached into his pocket and gave generously to the man. Then with a new mysterious energy within him Francis took the hand of the leprous man and pressed it to his lips. He kissed him. This was a whole new depth to his conversion. Not only had he encountered personally the love of God in his heart, and known the indescribable joy of the presence of the Spirit of Jesus within him. Now he was experiencing the love of God flowing through him for this outcast and marginalised man. The grace of practical love for the poor was born in him. Francis would never be the same again. By God's grace he had passed through a barrier that very few in his society were prepared to cross. It was normal that lepers should be shunned and kept at a distance. And this conversion to the poor was not just a moment of emotionally impulsive mercy that would evaporate the next day. From that time onwards he spent many days in the leper colony, providing for them, praying with them and even in some instances bringing physical healing.

In the vicinity of Assisi at "rivo torto" (bend in the river), there is a beautiful church within which there is a replica of the first humble dwelling of Francis and his brothers – a cowshed. One of the stained glass windows depicts the scene of Francis meeting the leper on the road. Outside the church there is a life-size bronze statue of Francis kneeling and washing the body of another leprous man, whose face shows signs of deep distress. It captures powerfully a moment when the brothers had been caring for suffering patients in a hospital.[6] The man in question had been angry and irritable with his condition and shouting blasphemies at the brothers such that they were feeling unable to help him. Coming upon this pitiable scene Francis asked the man what he wanted. The man replied by cursing the brothers and demanding to be washed because of the stink of his wretched sores which he couldn't stand any longer. Then Francis, with great tenderness, gently washed his sores with scented water. Wherever Francis touched the man his wounds were healed. As the man began to see the healing taking place in his body he started weeping for his sins. Not only was he cleansed bodily but also he was cleansed of all his leprosy of soul which was even more deadly.

True Gospel Poverty

I have related the key elements of Francis' early conversion experience because they illustrate the call to evangelical poverty. This is at the heart of the gospel, but often those who present themselves to the world as preachers of the gospel overlook its importance. In our present culture people highly value possession of wealth, luxury items and an opulent lifestyle. When Francis was touched deeply by the love of God, and persuaded by the power of the Cross, he freely and joyfully renounced material things so he could live for God alone. He wanted to imitate Jesus in his poverty.

We are indebted to Francis for the Christmas crib which speaks of God's preference for the poor and his identification with the poor. In 1223 at Greccio Francis was fasting and praying. He asked a wealthy man to put together a life-size replica of the scene at Bethlehem. There was a manger, and a live donkey and a cow.[7] Francis wanted to see, feel and touch the mystery of Bethlehem. He wanted people to really appreciate the humility of Jesus' birth into poverty. Francis had a deep sense of the incarnation, that God has become one of us, entering into our mess, and accepting and loving us there. Unfortunately in the modern era we have tended to sanitise the stable in Bethlehem and surround it with sentimentality. Rather it is an earthy symbol of how God has become one with our human predicament and shared the poverty of our broken condition. He did not come to a palace, but a stable in a cave hewn in the hillside, and he was laid in a manger, a trough for feeding animals. It is a robust call to change our lives and to embrace a simpler lifestyle, without greed and devoid of opulence. The love of God cannot really be in our hearts if we love all that the world craves. The life of Francis calls us back to desiring God above all things and finding him present in the weak, broken, lost, oppressed and marginalised in the society.

Poverty of Spirit

Francis also reminds us that we can receive the gift of the "nativity of the soul", a *spiritual* poverty which makes space for God made flesh to dwell within our hearts. Christ can be born in our hearts because he was born of Mary in Bethlehem. The Word of God first descended from his throne and his light entered into the darkness in extreme poverty, in silence and in peace. As we acknowledge our poverty God is drawn to dwell within our hearts and we can experience this nativity of the soul. He is born in us.

From the moment he heard the words spoken to him while praying before the San Damiano cross Francis was touched deeply by the love of Jesus expressed in his passion and death. Whenever he beheld a crucifix Francis would be reduced to tears. So much did he identify with the suffering of Jesus for the world. Towards the end of his life on Mount La Verna he experienced the wounds of Jesus on the cross being seared into his own body. Francis had prayed, "My Lord Jesus Christ, I pray you to grant me two graces before I die: the first is that during my life I may feel in my soul and in my body, as much as possible, that pain which you, dear Jesus, sustained in the hour of your most bitter passion. The second is that I may feel in my heart, as much as possible, that excessive love with which you, O Son of God, were inflamed in willingly enduring such suffering for us sinners". Wherever his brothers would go they would often pray, "We adore you, O Christ, and we bless you, because by your holy Cross you have redeemed the world".

This love for the Cross was at the heart of Francis' love for poverty. On the Cross Jesus was stripped of everything, reduced to nothing, hated, despised and rejected. The way of Jesus is that of abandonment, and the way of littleness. It is the way of humility. It is the way of being not annoyed or upset when people criticise us. It is the way of rejoicing when others speak against us, and it is the way of love for those who strike us in the face. The poverty of Jesus, modelled by Francis, rejects all prestige. We are often worried about how we look before others, our position and status in the evaluation of others. We want to be on a pedestal to be looked at and admired by all. Jesus says, "Anyone who wishes to be first among you must be the slave of all" (Mk 10:44). It is a journey towards being the least of all through being the servant of all. For Francis poverty of spirit is closely related to humility. In the canticle of the sun he extols water as "useful, humble, precious and pure". It is easy to see that water is useful, also it is precious, especially in desert lands, and pure because it is clear. But why would water be humble? Because it always runs to the lowest place! This is in imitation of God himself.

We have already seen how Francis sees this expressed in Bethlehem and on the Cross. In a letter to all the Friars he also speaks poetically of the Eucharist as God's humility:

> Our whole being should be seized with fear; the whole world should tremble and heaven rejoice, when Christ, the Son of the Living God, is present on the altar in the hands of the priest. What wonderful majesty! What stupendous condescension! O sublime humility! O humble sublimity! That the Lord of the whole universe, God and the Son of God, so humbles himself like this and hides under the form of a little bread, for our salvation.[8]

Francis goes on to encourage his Friars to humble themselves, and pour out their hearts before the Lord that they may be exalted by him (1 Peter 5:6). In the face of such humility on the Lord's part we must keep nothing for ourselves, "so that he who has given himself wholly to you may receive you wholly".

Evangelisation

Francis was a romantic. He knew he was being pursued by his divine Lover and he allowed himself to be won. Like Jeremiah he could well have said, "You seduced me, O Lord, and I allowed myself to be seduced" (Jer 20:7). His life was a love song to his Beloved. He delighted in drawing aside with his Beloved in solitude in the caves on Mount Subasio. His desire had been awakened, and now the flame of love in his heart was insatiable. It was a love that could not be contained. At first it was satisfied with restoring churches; the San Damiano, then another small building, and then the St Mary of the Angels, which eventually became his humble "headquarters". But this burning love, fed by his prayer, propelled him towards mission. A decisive moment came during a Mass at the Portiuncla. The priest was reading the text from Matthew's gospel: "Go, proclaim the good news, 'the kingdom of God is at hand!'....Freely you have received, freely give....Take no gold, or silver, or copper in your belts, no bag for your journey, nor two tunics, nor sandals, nor staff, for the labourer deserves his living. And whatever town or village you enter, find out who in it is worthy, and stay there until you leave. As you enter the house greet it saying 'peace be to this house'" (Mt 10:6-11). These words struck a deep chord in his heart. For Francis this was the defining moment. In his testament before his death Francis remembers this day of decision when "the most High personally revealed to me that I ought to live according to the Holy Gospel".[9] He now saw himself as a "troubadour of the great King". This fire of love within him burst forth into mission. After asking the priest to explain the text to him, Francis exclaimed, "That is what I want! That is what I seek! I long to do that with all my heart!" He instantly threw away his staff, took off his shoes, and dispensed with his cloak. He kept only his tunic. He made himself a simple, rough garment, and discarding his leather belt, he tied a cord around his waist, and set forth to preach the gospel. No longer was he going to rebuild chapels; he was destined to restore the Church itself.

Being so madly in love with Jesus, Francis initially found it difficult to decide whether he was meant to spend his life mainly in solitude or to go out preaching the Good News. He sent Br Masseo to go to Clare to ask her to seek the Lord for a solution to his dilemma. He also sent a message to Br Sylvester who at that time was praying on Mount Subasio to beg for wisdom from God. They both sent back the same message to Francis: "The Lord wants you to go about the world preaching because God did not call you for yourself alone but also for the salvation of others".[10] This settled it for Francis. The solitudes were where the flame of God's love was stoked, generating the fire for preaching. After a long time alone with the Lord, soaking up his love, and allowing their hearts to be purified by this love, Francis and his friars would go forth boldly to proclaim Christ who was their first love.

They were not versed in doctrine or apologetics; nor did they indulge in protracted sermons. They proclaimed a simple message of repentance, assuring their listeners of the love and mercy of God, and calling them to change their hearts, rejecting evil ways and turning to the good. It was *kerygmatic* preaching similar to what we find related in Acts of the Apostles. After Pentecost the apostles simply proclaimed Jesus crucified who is now Lord, and called all to faith and repentance. Likewise, this new wave of evangelisation, under the fire of the Holy Spirit focussed on the same basic gospel message. Gone were the erudite and complex orations of the sermons of the day. Now a simple message of salvation won in Jesus Christ cut to the hearts of the listeners. Thomas of Celano tells us:

> Francis again and again declared that nothing was to be preferred to this labour for the salvation of souls, because Christ has deigned to hang on the Cross for them. For this the constant wrestling of the saint in prayer, his zeal for preaching, the excess of his good example. He would not have deemed himself a friend of Christ had he not loved the souls which Christ has loved.

What made their proclamation so powerful was their way of life. It was not theory, but an invitation to a new way to change the world. At the beginning they were just so full of joyful simplicity which they had found to be such a liberating experience for their hearts that they just wanted everyone to know that there is a new way to live. When Francis and Giles made their first journey Francis would sing out in French, praising and blessing the Lord in a loud voice for all in the market place to hear. He would urge the people to open their hearts to the love of God, to fear him and to turn away from their sins. Giles would back him up with "What he says is right! Believe him!"[11] When people would ask them who they were, at first they were not quite sure how to answer. But eventually they simply answered, "We are the penitents from Assisi".

The most famous of Francis' evangelising missions was his encounter with Al-Malik al-Kamil, the Muslim sultan ruler of Damietta in the Holy Land. The Crusader armies were preparing for a major assault on Damietta. Francis had felt called to make the dangerous journey to the front lines. Being a man of peace he was not interested in the military exercise, but simply wanted to meet the sultan and tell him about Jesus. Instead of encouraging the soldiers to kill others for the sake of liberating the Holy Land, Francis proposed a bold alternative. Why not go and talk to the sultan and convince him about the Good News of God's love? Rather than seek to cut the throats of the Saracens and defeat them by force why not persuade them with love? Taking a brother with him Francis approached the enemy lines; poor, barefoot, unpretentious. They were immediately seized by the Muslims, who began to manhandle them. Francis kept repeating, "The sultan! The sultan!"

Somewhat bemused by this inoffensive friar, they hauled them before the sultan. Rather than order instant death the sultan seems to have been intrigued by the arrival of the friars. To make fun of them the sultan had laid in front of them a large carpet covered with crosses. If they walked on the carpet they would be trampling on the cross, but if they did not they would be insulting the sultan. Francis immediately began walking over the carpet towards the sultan, who began mocking him for trampling on the Christian cross. Francis simply replied, "There were three crosses on Calvary, one was the Cross of Christ which we revere; the other two were of robbers; they are yours and we have no scruples in treading upon them". Francis and the sultan quickly became friends, each respecting the other as they discussed their differences.

Some testimonies speak of Francis inviting the sultan and

his advisors to a test by fire. He asked for a furnace to be lit. He proclaimed boldly that the authentic bearer of truth would walk through the fire unscathed. Faced with this challenging proposal of the poor man from Assisi the sultan's advisers were gripped by fear and quickly disappeared. Then Francis offered to walk through the fire on one condition. If he was protected by God the sultan was to promise to acknowledge Christ as Saviour and Lord. But the sultan had to admit that, even if that miraculous proof was given, he could not change his religion. Francis was disappointed but resigned to failure. He had done all he could to persuade Al-Malik al- Kamil, but the sultan was bound to his Muslim faith and could not change. Nevertheless, Francis' courage in proclaiming the gospel will be remembered always. They departed friends. The sultan wanted to bestow many gifts on Francis, but the poor man of Assisi only accepted an "oliphant", a sort of horn, which Francis used later when he was calling people to hear him preach.

Brotherhood

After each preaching expedition the friars would return to the brotherhood and share with one another their experiences of the apostolate. This was the same dynamic as Jesus with his apostles. We are told Jesus called his apostles firstly "to be with him" and then he "sent them" out to preach the kingdom of God and bring healing (Mk 3:16). They were to be with Jesus in prayer and brotherhood first, and then to be sent out to preach the gospel. Being brothers together gave the mutual support they needed in their demanding ministry, earthing them from becoming over spiritualised, and was in itself a witness of love, showing a new way to live the gospel through kindness, poverty, generosity, reconciliation, joy and peace.

We cannot underestimate the importance of brotherhood for Francis. He loved the brothers and his whole mission flowed out of brotherhood. It was a crucible for learning practical love, humility, forgiveness and reconciliation. Many stories have been told of their brotherly love. In Assisi when they were begging for food sometimes people would treat them like mad men and throw stones at them. The brothers would vie with one another to be the one to be hit by the stone and so protect the other brothers. In his writings Francis urged his brothers to live with one another according to the principles of the gospel. There was to be no slander or detraction. The tongue needed to be in control: "Rather than speaking evil of one another, the friars should be glad to serve and obey one another in a spirit of charity".[12] They were to avoid envy: "When a man envies his brother because of what the good God does or says through him, it is like committing a sin of blasphemy, because it is really envying God who is the source of every good".[13]

They were to be patient with one another's shortcomings. Patience is tested, Francis says, when those who should cooperate with a brother do the exact opposite. This is when a brother knows how patient he really is.[14] Brothers should never take offence due to an injury done by another, but be ready to forgive.[15] They are not to be scandalized when another brother falls. If a brother is "upset or angry for any reason other than charity he is only drawing blame upon himself".[16] They were to greet one another joyfully and with affection. They were to be hospitable to the stranger at all times. They were to care for the sick amongst them and not to abandon them no matter what the circumstances.[17] He says, "Blessed is the brother who loves his brother as much when he is sick and of no use to him as when he is well and can be of use to him".[18]

Francis was particularly strong in insisting that "all friars without exception are forbidden to wield power or authority, particularly over one another".[19] He quotes the gospel where Jesus corrects his apostles: "You know that among the Gentiles those whom they recognise as their rulers lord it over them, and their great ones are tyrants over them. But it is not so among you; but whoever wishes to be first among you must be slave of all" (Mk 10:42-43). Those who are elected "ministers" in the brotherhood must be genuinely humble servants in imitation of Jesus.[20] What is notable about the various rules of Francis is that while he calls brothers to religious obedience, he is much more intent on calling those who have authority to exercise it in imitation of Jesus, who took up towel and water, the position of the slave to wash the feet of the apostles. Francis knew that obedience will be inspired when authority is exercised with love and humility.

Mercy

Francis never lost the sweetness of the impact of his first encounter with the leper. His proclamation of the gospel always included compassion for the poor, and healing for those who were afflicted in any way. A beautiful story in the *Little Flowers* illustrates this.[21] Dangerous robbers roamed the countryside in the area where the brothers lived. One day when Francis was out begging, a well-known robber came to the door of the Friary asking for food. The guardian, Angelo, refused, and rebuked him for his criminal behaviour, saying he did not deserve to eat food which had been given to the friars. On his return Francis was aghast at the way the guardian had treated the man: "You acted in a cruel way, because sinners are led back to God by holy gentleness rather than cruel scolding. For our Master Jesus Christ, whose Gospel we have promised to observe, says that the doctor is not needed by those who are well but by the sick, and 'I have come to call not the just but sinners to repentance', and therefore he often ate with them." Francis ordered Angelo to take the bread and wine which he had just begged and go out to the nearby mountains and valleys and search for the robbers until he found them. He was then to offer them the bread and wine, and kneel before them and ask for forgiveness for not respecting their dignity and offending them. Then he was to ask them in the name of Francis "not to do these evil things any more, but to fear God, and not to offend their neighbours". He was to promise them that, if they do so, Francis would make sure they are provided for with food and drink all the time.

While the guardian was carrying out these orders, Francis began to pray and beg the Lord to soften the hearts of the robbers and bring them to repentance. As a result, when Angelo finally found the robbers and discharged his mission, their hearts were opened and they began to see the foolishness of their ways, and were convicted of their sinfulness. They began to compare their evil life with the holiness of the friars. They were filled with the fear of God, and loss of their souls. They were so convinced of their helpless plight that they decided to go to Francis and ask for forgiveness and seek his advice on what they should do. Francis welcomed them with affection and consoled them with stories of God's mercy. He promised them God would have mercy on them because Christ came into the world to redeem sinners. All three repented and joined the friars, being faithful until death.

Love for Creation

One of the most popular and endearing qualities of Francis was his communion with all living creatures and indeed with the whole of creation. He preached to the birds, exhorting them, "you must always and everywhere praise Him, because he has given you freedom to fly anywhere...Therefore, my little bird sisters, be careful not to be ungrateful, but strive always to praise God."[22] By courageous gentleness he tamed the ferocious wolf of Gubbio which had been terrorising the town, brokering a peace pact whereby "brother wolf" promised not to harass the villagers and in return was assured to receive daily food from them.[23] Francis communed with all creation, even preaching to the flowers, "inviting them to praise the Lord, just as if they were endowed with reason".[24] He would call creatures, no matter how insignificant, "brother" or "sister". Pope Francis points out that Francis' radical poverty was not just an ascetical practice, but also a deep awareness that everything is gift from God, and consequently he refused to misuse or manipulate creation for his own ends. His communion with nature reminds us in our technological age of the danger of exploiting creation irresponsibly. Francis calls us back to a gratitude for the gift of creation, affection for all creatures and a sense of awe and wonder at the beauty that surrounds us, as well as a wise and responsible attitude in caring for "our common home" on planet earth.[25]

The Stigmata

While Francis of Assisi remains popular amongst people from all different religious persuasions, and diverse ethnic and cultural groupings, relatively few realise that the key to his life is found in the Cross of Jesus. He can be extolled for his ecological awareness, his joyful disposition, his way of making peace and reconciling others, his simplicity of heart and love for all men and women. But all of these are the good fruit of his imitation of Jesus, not by following a distant gospel ideal, but through an abiding union with Jesus crucified. Towards the end of his life on Mount Alverna his mystical union with Jesus was consummated; his body was pierced through with the very wounds of Jesus, giving him an intimate share in the sufferings of our Saviour.[26] As Paul said, "the marks on my body are those of Jesus" (Gal 6:17). For Paul, of course, the wounds were inflicted by floggings, persecution and imprisonment which he endured in his apostolate. For Francis it was a mystical experience of being joined with Jesus on the Cross. But it also had a practical bite to it.

For Francis perfect joy was only to be found in the Cross. His instruction to Br Leo on this topic is challenging.[27] They were returning home amidst the snow on a bitterly cold day and Francis began to ask what would bring true joy to them. He suggests a number of possibilities; for example – that they perform the same miracles as Jesus did, or that they have extraordinary knowledge and the gift of prophecy, or that they could preach with the voice of angels, and convert all their hearers. But none of these he says would bring perfect joy. Leo is full of wonder and begs, "Tell me then where is perfect joy to be found?" Francis replies that it would come if they arrived home to find that the brother at the door rejects them and casts them out into the snow and rain, cold and hungry. And then if they came back and knocked again they were abused and set upon with clubs and beaten half to death. If they endured these sufferings and humiliations in union with the suffering of Jesus they would have true joy. He says , "we cannot glory in all those marvellous gifts of God, as they are not ours but God's...but we can glory in the cross of tribulations and afflictions, because that is ours, and so Paul the apostle says: 'I will glory in nothing but the Cross of our Lord Jesus Christ'".

Consumed by passionate love for his Saviour, Francis shared physically in his passion. This was a robust love, far removed from the sentimental, romanticised versions of his life that hagiographers can sometimes present. This was a love that knew no bounds. His imitation of Jesus' poverty was such that at the end of his journey he wanted to be stripped naked and left on the bare ground to express that he brought nothing at all to God, but a will totally given in love.

CLARE OF ASSISI

Chronology

1193 - Born in Assisi in a noble family

1212 - on Palm Sunday leaves family home to join Francis

1215 - becomes abbess at San Damiano

1216 - Pope Innocent grants privilege of poverty

1240 - Saracens invade San Damiano

1253 - dies on August 11 at San Damiano

Quotes

We become what we love and who we love shapes what we become.

Our labour here is brief, but the reward is eternal. Do not be disturbed by the clamour of the world, which passes like a shadow. Do not let the false delights of the world deceive you.

Place your mind before the mirror of eternity!
Place your soul in the brilliance of glory!

And transform your entire being into the image of God through contemplation. Love God with all your heart, and also his Son Jesus, crucified for us. May the memory of him never leave your mind.

CLARE OF ASSISI

About eight years after Francis had the life-changing revelation from the crucifix in the San Damiano church, a remarkable event took place which rocked the nobility of Assisi and set tongues wagging throughout the town. On Palm Sunday 1212 the nineteen year old daughter of the famous house of Offreducio, abandoned her family to join Francis. To avoid the opposition of her family Clare stole away in the middle of the night.[28] To be able to escape she had first to lift enormous beams that held a hidden door in place, which was usually only opened to carry out the dead. Miraculously she found the power to do so. Together with her accomplice, cousin Pacifica, she was greeted by two brothers with flaming torches and they quickly made their way to the church of St Mary of the Angels where Francis was expectantly waiting. Upon arrival what had already been planned took place. At the altar of the little church Francis cropped off Clare's beautiful golden tresses as a sign that now she was totally given to God for her whole life.[29] Filled with unquenchable ardour Clare rejoiced that from this moment she belonged to God alone. The fire of God's love had consumed her heart and she wanted nothing else but to follow Francis in making Jesus her lifelong passionate desire.

Consecrated to the Lord

Clare, like Francis, was a romantic. Probably she first heard of Francis when she was about six years old and her family were sharing the latest gossip of this crazy son of Peter Bernadone who had dramatically shed his clothes in the public square before Bishop Guido. As she grew into her teenage years she became entranced by Francis' love for God. She had heard him preach in San Rufino cathedral on how God's love is enough for us. Her heart was won. Meeting secretly with Francis to talk about the things of God, she was more and more drawn to a deeper journey with Jesus. She was ready to forsake everything for her Saviour. Her flight from the family home was not a teenage whim or a momentary rush of excitement for adventure. It was a thoroughly considered plan carefully formulated and courageously executed, fully aware of the ire that it would arouse in her family. Nothing else but the madness of love could explain this daring escapade and its life-long consequences.

After Clare had made her consecration to the Lord, Francis immediately took her to the Benedictine nuns two miles away at Isola Romana. Even though she shared the same spirit as Francis it would not be appropriate for her to stay with the brothers. The convent she entered was for the rich, who had their own servants. Since she desired to renounce all worldly privileges Clare asked refuge in the convent as a servant. She came as one of the poor, not according to her status as a member of a noble family. Her relatives, realising they had been tricked, came in hot pursuit of this runaway teenager. Clare received them in the chapel of the convent, clinging to the altar cloth. We are told "they employed violent force, poisonous advice and flattering promises, trying to persuade her to give up such a worthless deed that was unbecoming to her class and without precedent in her family".[30] Their arguments had no effect. To convince them of her determination she pulled off the veil to reveal her shorn head. After a few days of harassment the relatives finally retreated, admitting defeat in the face of such madness. What annoyed them most was that Clare, who had already been in possession of her dowry, had sold her inheritance before leaving the family home, and given the money to the poor. They now were trying to persuade her to let them redeem the goods at a higher price. But she resisted their pleas since she did not want to cheat the poor. That foolhardiness was too much for them to bear.

Another Fool for God

To make matters worse for the family, sixteen days later Clare's sister, Agnes, also ran away from the family home to join Clare, and cousin Pacifica, who had now both been transferred by Francis to the monastery of Sant'Angelo in Panza. With another, even younger daughter fleeing from the world, the family were absolutely enraged. Uncle Monaldo, who was the family strong man, with twelve horsemen at his side, arrived at the monastery intent upon retrieving the fugitive.[31] They seized Agnes and were physically carrying her off, while the young girl anxiously pleaded with Clare to do something to help. Clare simply knelt to the ground and prayed fervently. With this plea to heaven the girl's body became so heavy they had to put her down and they could no longer lift her leaden body from the ground. Monaldo was so irate that he went to slap Agnes in the face, but a horrendous pain seared through his arm, and he screamed in agony. Clare caught up with them and demanded they release her sister. Soundly beaten by the power of prayer the assailants retreated, realising that they were trying to combat forces beyond their control.

Francis cut off Agnes' hair and received her profession. Now there were three members of this little band, who people later called the "Poor Ladies" or the "Poor Clares". Bishop Guido of Assisi who had befriended Francis took the women under his wing and offered them San Damiano as a refuge. Clare was Francis' "dear little spiritual plant", and he assured the sisters that the brothers would always support them by sharing with them whatever food they were able to beg. The self-sacrifice which Clare and her sisters embraced out of love for God is astonishing. They were enclosed within the walls of their convent, very rarely to step outside, and if so only for a short journey to visit the brothers down in the valley below. We have the record of one famous visit of Clare to the Portiuncla. Apparently she had persisted in asking Francis for the visit over a couple of years. Finally he conceded and Clare was invited to a meal at St Mary of the Angels. She came first to pray in the church and then was shown around the friary. Then she and Francis sat down to table together with all the other brothers. Francis began to share about the beauty of God and his ways in the world with such spiritual animation that Clare and everyone present went into rapture with their eyes and hands lifted up to heaven. They were interrupted by some of the citizens of Assisi who had rushed upon them with consternation. Apparently they had seen from the distance a fire burning as if the whole forest had become a blazing inferno. Arriving on the scene they only found Francis and Clare and their companions in prayer totally captive to the love of God.[32]

Penitential Life

Francis and his companions would visit their enclosed sisters to preach. On one celebrated occasion Francis arrived to preach the word of God to the sisters who were assembled in their little chapel. He first looked to heaven and preached Christ in his normal fashion. Then he had some ashes brought to him. He spread part of the ashes on the floor in a circle around him, and the rest he sprinkled on his bowed head. For a long time Francis knelt silently within the circle of ashes. Then straightening up he began to recite the Miserere (Psalm 51). Upon finishing the prayer he immediately left the chapel. This prophetic action moved the sisters deeply. By dramatic gesture, together with the words of the psalm, Francis had called them to repentance, reminding them that they came from dust and unto dust they will return.[33]

Clare and her sisters lived a penitential life. Characteristic of the age Clare regarded the severe mortification of the flesh as the way to holiness. However, in her devotion to Christ it seems that she was tempted beyond the limits that Francis himself would impose on his brothers. There are two recorded times when Francis had to curb her zeal for exotic penitential practices. In her initial fervour Clare slept on a bed of vine branches and sometimes on the bare floor with her head resting on a stone. However, this led to sickness and Francis intervened commanding her to at least have a sack of straw for a mattress. She was also accustomed to eat very little. Three days a week she did not eat anything, and on the other days she ate only bread and water. The sisters wondered how she stayed alive. In fact the severe fasting caused her to become seriously ill, so Francis again came to the rescue and ordered her to eat something every day. However, while Clare may have been tempted to excess in discipline, her biographers make it clear that her penances and privations in no way soured her soul or made her miserable to live with. Rather, she was filled with joy. As Thomas of Celano says, "Indeed the sufferings of the flesh made her rejoice, because they alleviated the weariness of heart".

Contemplation

Clare's life was dedicated to prayer. We are told "she was very diligent and solicitous in prayer, contemplation and the exhortation of her sisters. She had given her whole life to this."[34] She prayed day and night. She would rise at midnight and wake up the other sisters by touching them in silence, calling them to vigilance in prayer. She particularly liked to pray the hour of Sext, celebrated at noon, since the gospels tell us that the Lord was nailed to the cross at that hour. While she was committed to the many liturgical hours of the prayer of the Church which were said in common, her heart was constantly in interior communion with the Lord. She had received a contemplative grace. Renouncing the things of this world she was seeking to empty herself of earthly attachments so that she could encounter the living God.

Her whole way of life which was radically frugal and ascetic was simply a way of being with God alone. He was her joy, and no other earthly treasure could take his place. Her long days in the grinding routine of her little convent were not monotonous. This rhythm of life was the way that her soul could be ceaselessly given to prayer. Contemplation was not only an extraordinary heavenly activity separated from the ordinary chores of life. Rather the spirit of prayer and praise of God suffused her whole life, filling the humble, humdrum daily chores and indispensible tasks of her convent life. She simply lived in the presence of God at all times. The last words of the blessing she left to her sisters express it well: "May the Lord be with you at all times! And may you be always in Him!" In her Rule she urges her sisters, "While working, never let the spirit of prayer and devotion be extinguished, which all other temporal things must serve". Prayerful contemplation was to be so natural a part of their lives that it should become like the air one breathes.

Word Made Flesh

Clare shared Francis' deep love for the incarnation. There was one time on Christmas Eve when she was seriously ill and unable to move from her bed in order to go to the chapel. So all the sisters went as usual to Matins and left her alone. Clare complained to the Lord that she had been deprived of the joy of being able to celebrate his birth. Then she immediately began to hear the organ, responsories and the entire Office of the brothers in the church of St Mary of the Angels, as if she was present there. The church was too far away for her to hear even if they had modern means of amplification. Yet to her great delight, by the grace of God, she was even given to see the crib of the Lord which had been set up in the Church. The *Little Flowers* account of this event develops the story even further. It has Clare being miraculously carried to the church for Matins and Midnight Mass, experiencing the whole liturgy, including receiving Holy Communion, and then being carried back to bed.[35] Whatever about the facts it remains clear that the Christmas event was fundamental in Clare's spirituality. In the Rule she wrote: "Out of love for the most holy and most beloved Child, wrapped in poor little covers, laid in a manger, and for love of his most holy Mother, I admonish, plead and encourage my sisters that they always wear the poorest garments".

Once the Saracens, who were Muslims without respect for the Christian faith, were scaling the walls of the San Damiano Convent with intent to plunder and rape the sisters.[36] These mercenaries in the service of Frederick II had no respect for consecrated women. Clare was sick in bed. The sisters were terrified. In desperation, but with serene confidence, Clare ordered them to bring the Blessed Sacrament in a silver container. She had them carry her outside on her bed to confront the attackers, as she prayed to her Saviour, "Lord Jesus, do not allow these defenceless virgins to fall into the hands of these pagans. Protect them; for I, who have nourished them with your love, can do nothing for them". She gained an immediate assurance from the Lord that he would protect them. Encouraging her sisters she said, "I assure you daughters you will be saved; you have nothing to fear". As she held up the Blessed Sacrament before the men approaching the sisters, the assailants were suddenly thrown into confusion. Filled with fear they hastily clambered back over the walls and fled. Once again, in time of peril the power of Clare's prayer prevailed.

Crucified Lord

Likewise in union with Francis, she had a passionate devotion to Jesus crucified. One of her sisters recalled that Clare had "instructed her always to have the Lord's passion in her memory".[37] She used to get the sisters to pray the Office of Francis which was really a meditation on the spiritual experience of the passion of Jesus, and also the Prayer of the Five Wounds, which focussed more upon the physical sufferings of Jesus. Thomas of Celano tells us:

> Crying over the Lord's passion was well known to her. At times, she poured out feelings of bitter myrrh at the sacred wounds. At times she imbibed sweeter joys. The tears over the suffering Christ made her quite inebriated and her memory continually pictured him whom love had imprinted upon her heart.[38]

The letters of Clare to Agnes of Bohemia reveal the essence of her spirituality. Agnes was a princess who had been promised as a bride to various princes and kings. She had always refused to marry them, renouncing the privileges it would bring. In 1236 at the age of thirty-one she entered the monastery of San Salvatore in Prague which she, as a princess, had founded herself. In Clare's fourth letter to Agnes we find Clare urging her protege to embrace Christ as her Spouse and to rejoice in being the bride of Christ. She encourages Agnes to fix her sights upon the radiant Christ, who is like a mirror into which we can gaze. In this way she will see her true self and be formed more and more into the image of Christ himself. In the mirror she is to especially see Christ in Bethlehem and Christ on the Cross.

> Dearest beloved, on looking into that mirror, with the grace of God, you will be able to savour delights. Approach it and you will see there first Jesus asleep in the crib, his extreme poverty, his miserable swaddling clothes. O astounding poverty! O marvellous poverty! The King of the Angels, the Lord of Heaven and Earth, lying in a manger! In the middle of this

mirror, behold the blessed poverty of holy humility. For the redemption of the human race, it made him endure untold sufferings and hardships.[39]

Clare then goes on to direct Agnes to look deeper into the mirror and she will contemplate Jesus crucified: "The indescribable love which compelled Jesus to suffer on the wood of the Cross and to die there the most shameful death".[40] Her language is reminiscent of St Paul who says, "The love of Christ compels us if we think that if one man has died for all, then all should be dead" (2 Cor 5:14). In a previous letter she had encouraged Agnes to look upon her crucified Spouse and contemplate how "the most beautiful of the sons of men became the ugliest of men for our salvation, his body torn and rent by scourging" and how he expired on the Cross in extreme suffering. Contemplation of the passion of Jesus enflames the heart with love and inspires us to imitate Jesus in his sufferings. Agnes had already embraced the suffering of Jesus in renouncing honour, privilege and temporal wealth, choosing rather to live with humiliation, lowliness and poverty. She was now to burn with ardent love for her Saviour, to allow him to draw her into his inner chamber, and be embraced by his loving arms (cf Song of Songs 1:4).

The Privilege of Poverty

The Holy Spirit is forever creative, birthing fresh expressions of evangelical spirituality within the Church. Adhering faithfully to the spirit of Francis, his sister Clare devised a new way to be in religious community. It was common wisdom in the Church of the Middle Ages that consecrated women living together would need a regular source of income to keep them from destitution. Clare's inspiration flew directly in the face of this prevailing ecclesiastical assumption. She felt called to an enclosed, contemplative life with other sisters, relying totally on the providence of God without any revenues from properties and not even from their own work. All her sisters were equally sharing in the work of the convent with their spinning of cloth and subsistence gardening. Clare herself was constantly at the spinning wheel when not at prayer or recreation. But whatever they produced was always given away – garments for the poor, and vestments and altar cloths for the parishes. They sought no remuneration. Their trust was totally in God's gracious provision. They lived radically according to the gospel, when Jesus said, "Therefore I tell you, do not worry about your life, what you are to eat, or about your body, what you are to wear…..Consider the ravens, they neither sow nor reap, they have neither storehouse nor barn, and yet God feeds them. O how much more valuable you are than the birds!" (Luke 12:24-27)

Clare spent her whole life fighting for the "privilege of poverty", which in effect was the privilege to have no privileges. It guaranteed a life with no guarantees. She fought for the right and the privilege to be able to live absolute poverty. Even the work of their own hands the sisters gave away to the poor rather than sell for their own gain. This was how they lived; relying totally on what the local people or passers-by may give to them, trusting that the Lord would send what was needed without having to advertise their needs or to promote their cause before others.

Church Approval

Trouble came when she sought to gain juridical endorsement of this radical way of life. After many rebuffs and attempts by sympathetic ecclesiastics to persuade them to ameliorate their rule, Clare finally won the day with Pope Innocent III. He put in writing everything she so ardently desired:

> As is evident, you have renounced the desire for all temporal

things, desiring to dedicate yourselves to the Lord alone. Because of this, since you have sold all things and given them to the poor, you propose not to have possessions whatsoever, clinging in all things to the footprints of Him, the Way the Truth and the Life, Who, for your sake was made poor. Nor does a lack of possessions frighten you from a proposal of this sort; for the left hand of the heavenly Spouse is under your head to support the weakness of your body, which you have placed under the law of your soul through an ordered charity. Finally, he who feeds the birds of the heavens and clothes the lilies of the field will not fail you in either food or clothing, until He ministers to you in heaven, when His right hand especially will more happily embrace you in the fullness of His beatific vision. Therefore, we confirm with our apostolic authority, as you requested your proposal of most high poverty, granting you by the authority of this letter that no one can compel you to receive possessions.[41]

This solemn sanctioning of their way of life by the Pope brought intense joy to Clare. She wanted to have a community of sisters who had no financial or material security, radically relying on the Lord for his provision. Her love for absolute poverty was at the core of her love for God and desire to be for him alone. We can easily see the correlation here with the ideal of Francis. In his Testament towards the end of his life Francis says:

> When God gave me some friars, there was no one to tell me what I should do; but the most High himself made it clear to me that I must live the life of the Gospel. I had this written down briefly and simply and his holiness the Pope confirmed it for me. Those who embraced this life gave everything they had to the poor. They were satisfied with one habit which was patched inside and outside, and a cord, and trousers. We refused to have anything more.[42]

In the early days Francis and his companions worked in the fields for their keep. Refusing to take money in remuneration they happily received some food as an alternative. When there was not enough food coming from their labours they would go out begging for the love of God. So in this regard Clare and her sisters were even more radical than Francis, since they did not take any recompense at all for their work and neither did they actively beg. They simply waited trustingly upon the hand of the Lord to feed them.

DOMINIC GUZMAN

Chronology

1170 - born at Caleruega, Spain

1201 - sub-prior at Osma

1203 - meeting with the Catharist inn-keeper

1206 - launch of the preaching mission in absolute poverty

1215 - Dominic and brothers open a house in Toulouse

1217 - confirmation by Innocent III of the order of preachers. Sending out of brothers

1221 - dies on August 6 at Bologna, Italy

Quotes

A man who governs his passions is master of his world.
We must either command them or be enslaved by them.
It is better to be a hammer than an anvil.

The seed will go mouldy and rot if it is hoarded up;
it will be fruitful if it is sown widely

Arm yourself with prayer rather than a sword;
wear humility rather than fine clothes.

Come let us worship and fall down before God;
let us weep before the God who made us.

Have charity one for another;
Guard humility;
Make your treasure out of voluntary poverty.

DOMINIC

Born somewhere around 1171 into a noble Castilian family in the village of Caleruega in Spain, Dominic was soon to be given to the Church. While he was still in the womb his mother had a vision of her child as a small dog with a lighted torch in its jaws. She sensed her child was destined to set the world on fire.[43] Later she saw on her young son's forehead a shining moon or star. These signs, Jordan of Saxony relates, presaged what was to come – the birthing of a vocation to preach with the same fire which Jesus had come to bring to the earth (Lk 12:49). At the age of seven Dominic was placed by his family in a type of primary school specifically designed to train young men to be clerics. At the age of fourteen he then was sent to College at Palencia, where he made the New Testament his staple reading, committing large portions of Scripture to memory. Using the commentaries of the Fathers of the Church, he carefully studied the text, copying notes in the margin of his parchment bible. His knowledge of the gospels deepened, and he would spend long hours in silence and solitude. Already from an early age we see the shape of Dominic's later vocation – "prayer and service of the word" (Acts 6:4).

The young Dominic Guzman, like his contemporary, Francis of Assisi, had a predilection for evangelical poverty. Even as a youth studying in Palencia an incident occurred which showed his maturing in gospel living well beyond his years. In the midst of a great famine in Spain he was surrounded by people starving to death. Without hesitation he sold all of his beloved books, which were absolutely indispensable for a budding cleric, so he could give all the money to the poor. He was already becoming committed to the way of poverty which was to reach its fulfilment in later years.

Prayer and Study

When he was around 24 years old Dominic was invited by Don Diego de Azevedo, the Prior of the Cathedral Chapter at Osma, to join the community. A few months after joining the Chapter he was ordained a priest. The Chapter involved a communal way of life according to the rule of St Augustine. The clerics shared their possessions and divided their time between singing the hours of the Office, personal contemplative prayer, preaching to the faithful, and offering the sacrifice of the Mass. It was an apostolic life within community. The priests were called Canons Regular, and the usual attire was a white tunic with a black coat and hood, which eventually became the basis for the Dominican habit. Yet at this stage Dominic had no aspirations towards founding a congregation. He was simply seeking personal holiness through prayer, the word of God, and growing in virtue. He was especially dedicated to prayer. Accustomed to all night vigils he was often found rapt in wordless communion with God and occasionally bursting out with cries of joyful praise.

After six years of this rhythm of prayer and study of God's word as a Canon, Dominic was invited by Diego, who had now been appointed his bishop, to join him on a journey to Scandinavia, then known as Dacia. Diego had been charged by the King of Castile to be the royal ambassador in negotiating the marriage of the prince to a Scandinavian princess. This rather secular mission became a turning point in the lives of both Diego and Dominic. As they passed through the south of France they encountered the scourge of heresy that was confusing simple people and causing them to renounce their Catholic faith. They could see how the Church was desperately in need of reform, since its institutions were wedded to the ruling class and the clergy had lost credibility with the ordinary folk in the lower classes.

Bishops were often feudal overlords, related to powerful families. Kings were dependent on clerics to staff their civil service, and bishops were usually chosen from amongst these clerics. There were no seminaries. Consequently secular clergy, who were ordained to minister the sacraments, visit the sick and bury the dead, received very little training. They often lived dissolute lives, taking concubines, gambling, and producing unwanted children.

This compromised life of the clergy, together with the wedding of the Church to the elite, provided the dark background for the renewal sparked by Francis of Assisi and Dominic. Everywhere there had already been attempts to restore the Church to its primitive evangelical beauty. Many movements seeking to live the gospel radically had sprung up spontaneously and were taking hold in the hearts of the people. Unfortunately, most of these had an anti-clerical flavour, and many of them were heretical. Francis and Dominic, responded to the crisis of their times differently. They saw clearly that the Church's credibility was compromised, but while championing a new, more authentic way to live the gospel, they remained passionately submitted to Church authority, and retained a deep reverence for the priesthood.

The Cathari

One such "reform" movement was called the "Cathari", who appealed to the ordinary people, because of their austerities and detachment from the world. They were popularly called the "Albigensians" since it originated in the town of Albi in Languedoc in the south of France. The movement had four "bishops", dozens of deacons, and thousands of wandering *perfecti*, who were living the strict adherence of the ascetical practices of the sect. They went about preaching purity, carrying no money with them and dressed in a plain black tunic. It appeared to the undiscerning eye that these radical zealots were living the true gospel life and the Catholic bishops, who were accustomed to luxurious palaces and numerous servants, were charlatans.

The Cathari, like the Gnostics in the early Church and the Manichees of Augustine's time, were dualist in their view of the world. They taught that God is good, but the body is evil. While God made the spiritual part of humanity, the material world, including the human body, was made by the devil and is evil. They regarded humanity caught in a battle between the principles of good and evil, between the spiritual world and the material world. The only way to holiness is to get out of the body, and that can only happen through extravagant forms of asceticism, which free the soul from imprisonment in the body. This false teaching denied the incarnation, since according to their thinking, God could not have become a man and hence be subject to Satan. Christ was only a divine messenger, one of the highest angels. Salvation can only be obtained by freeing yourself from slavery to the created world.

Consecrated in the Truth

Dominic's first head-on encounter with this mentality was in a tavern in Toulouse when he discovered to his dismay that his host was a convinced Catharist. Dominic engaged the inn keeper in debate which went through the night. By morning he had the joy of seeing the man renounce his errors and pledge his belief in the truth. No doubt, during the argument that night, the seed was planted in Dominic's heart which was to later blossom in his life-long dedication to preaching the truth against the lies of the heretics, who were destroying the Church. This first encounter of Dominic with the danger of erroneous doctrine, was the beginning of a journey which was very much about being consecrated in the truth. In his long years of contemplation and study he had learnt to love the truth of the Scriptures and the teaching of the Church. Jesus prayed to the father for his disciples, "I am not asking you to take them out of the world, but to protect them from the evil one. They do not belong to the world any more than I belong to the world. Consecrate them in the truth; your word is truth" (John 17:15-17).

Dominic held the truths of the faith to be sacred; he had consecrated himself to Jesus, who is *the* Truth. He preached Jesus as our Saviour and Lord, who won our salvation by his death and resurrection; the heart of the gospel proclamation. The whole vast edifice of Catholic teaching finds its meaning from being centred around this core proclamation, which the New Testament calls the "kerygma". In defending the faith against heretics Dominic never contained himself only to apologetics, but proclaimed the fire of God's love revealed in Christ crucified. His conversions were undoubtedly supported by the cogency of his arguments against the heretics, but hearts were enflamed by the fire of the Spirit as Jesus was proclaimed, and his proclamation of the Good News was accompanied by miracles as Jesus had promised (Mk 16:20).

Upon arrival in Scandinavia (Dacia) Bishop Diego and Dominic discovered the young woman had decided to elude marriage by slipping off to a convent, thus beyond reach of her suitor without Papal intervention. This seems to be the main reason why Diego and his sub-prior then travelled hastily to Rome. But Diego also had an ulterior motive for going to Rome. After having encountered some of the victims of the barbarians of the North, and maybe even the barbarians themselves, Diego had decided to gain the approval of the Pope to launch an evangelising mission into Dacia. He and Dominic were appalled that so many people were totally ignorant of Christ. The Pope flatly refused to commission them on such a dangerous mission. Both men were not afraid of martyrdom; to the contrary, we know that Dominic had an intense desire to give his life for Christ.[44] Even after the Order began Dominic was keen to leave his administrative tasks to seek the ultimate goal of a martyr's death. But it was not in God's providential plan.

Inspiration from God

On their way back from Rome they visited Citeaux, where the Cistercian renewal of Benedictine monasteries had begun. Diego requested to be clothed in the monastic habit, probably so he could be identified more clearly with the mission to Languedoc which the Pope had entrusted to the Cistercians. So, together with some Cistercians, enlisted from Citeaux, Diego and Dominic returned to the south of France, where the Cathari were continuing to gain the upper hand. On arrival they met with Papal legates who had already been labouring in vain to combat the grip the heretics had upon the populace. These religious who had been commissioned by the Pope were now at their wit's end, and ready to throw in the towel. All three of them had decided to resign their posts. So much had been demanded of them and they were discouraged, having failed to win the people back to the faith.

Under the inspiration of the Holy Spirit, Diego and Dominic quickly sized up the situation. The heretics with their austere asceticism were attracting people because they had the appearance of holiness and simple gospel poverty. In direct contrast, the Papal legates had numerous servants, were riding on horses, wearing rich clothing and dining sumptuously. Diego challenged the legates to divest themselves of everything and go barefoot in preaching the gospel. The legates protested that this was impossible. To convince them Diego himself took the lead, sending his own retinue and his horses and belongings back to Osma, keeping only some books. Diego, with Dominic at his side, now became the leader of the preaching expedition, and this was quickly endorsed by Pope Innocent III, who allowed Diego to launch the new mission while he occasionally commuted between Languedoc and his diocese in Osma.

Credibility Restored

No longer could the missionaries be accused of empty talk as they set out to preach the truth on foot in voluntary poverty, carrying no possessions except some books considered necessary for prayer and study. No doubt they were able to identify with the commission of Jesus, "Do not turn your steps to pagan territory"; they had been denied the possibility of going to the barbarians, "go rather to the lost sheep of the House of Israel"; to those who belonged to the Church but were now lost to heretical ideas and practices.

> And as you go, proclaim that the kingdom of heaven is close at hand. Cure the sick, raise the dead, cleanse lepers, cast out devils. You received without charge, give without charge. Provide yourselves with no gold or silver, not even a few coppers for your purses, with no haversack for the journey or spare tunic or footwear or a staff, for the workman deserves his keep (Matthew 10:5-10).

They were happy to beg for their food and trust the Lord for his provision. This was the beginning of a new outpouring of the Holy Spirit. The people were won by the sincerity of the witness of Bishop Diego and Dominic. Prior to this the people heard the words of the papal legates but were not convinced; now the witness of their lives gave credibility to their words, and the Holy Spirit broke open the hearts of their listeners.

From that time onwards Dominic always travelled barefoot, but in a self-effacing manner. He would only take off his shoes when he was walking between towns on rough roads covered with mud, sharp stones or brambles. Once a friend of the heretics had maliciously misled Dominic and others on a wild goose chase through a dense forest with many obstacles which cost him and his friends dearly with their legs bleeding due to all the abrasions. At the end of the journey, Dominic, who had guessed that they had been tricked, shouted out with joy, "Beloved, have high hopes, for the Lord will give us victory. See, our sins are already washed away in blood". The heretic was completely overcome, and by God's grace was converted on the spot.

The preachers immediately gained significant break-throughs with the people. They held numerous disputes in the cities and the towns, confronting the Cathari in public debates. On one occasion at Fanjeaux, when both Dominic's presentation and that of the Cathari were highly persuasive, the judges decided to have a "trial by fire". Dominic's book was thrown into the flames and was not burnt. The text of the heretics caught fire instantly. Needless to say conversions of the people followed. For two years this band of Catholic missionaries, made up of Dominic, Bishop Diego, and a dozen or so Cistercians, continued to preach Christ throughout the region. The witness of Diego's magnetic personality, prodigious energy and moral integrity influenced many to come back to the faith.

A sign from God: Signadou

Diego conceived the idea of a convent to shelter young women who had grown up in the heretical culture, but now wanted to return to the Catholic faith. Their impoverished parents, even if they did not subscribe to the Cathari ideology, had out of necessity entrusted the education of these girls to the heretics. While the vision for the convent was probably initially conceived by Diego, the divine endorsement was received by Dominic. There was a church dedicated to the Blessed Virgin in Prouille, a village not far from Fanjeaux, a Catharist stronghold. Dominic often prayed in this church before the shrine of Our Lady. One night when he was at prayer on a hillside not far from the church he saw a globe of fire appear over the shrine. He took it as a sign from God, *Signadou*, that the convent they were hoping to establish would be at this holy place. Dominic brought together nine girls converted by his preaching. The young girls had been brought up by the *perfecti*, so they were open to a strong evangelical way of life. The women were to pray continually for the work of the preaching brothers of Dominic as the Order began to develop. They were dedicated to the education of young women imperilled by the Cathari, and engaged in a life of prayer and manual work.

Before the new community took possession of its home in December 1206 Bishop Diego had already returned to his diocese of Osma with the intention of gathering around him like-minded priests to be a preaching force to help with the work in France. But to the dismay of all, shortly after returning home he died suddenly, and went to the Lord for his eternal reward. The unexpected demise of his beloved mentor and guide grieved Dominic deeply. Adding to Dominic's disappointment was the disappearance from the mission of the Abbots and religious of Citeaux, and other priests who had come from Spain to help. He was left practically alone, yet unshaken, persevering in the work of preaching which God had given him. He never flagged in zeal and was fearless in facing his enemies. Gradually he attracted new co-workers who were not yet in obedience to him but shared his zeal for the conversion of the heretics. They were a little band of missionaries, called the "preaching brothers".

The Beginning

At last in 1215 Dominic was positioned to begin his new Order. He was forty five years old when this work began to take shape. In Toulouse two key wealthy citizens were waiting to help. They placed themselves and all they possessed at the disposal of Dominic. Peter Seila offered his house for the use of Dominic and his six companions. Dominic invested his men in the habit of the Canons Regular and they adopted a life of communal poverty and the discipline of personal contemplative prayer and singing the Office in common. They were to be dedicated to prayer and study of the word of God so they could preach the word of God with fire and the Holy Spirit. The study was particularly important; to be versed in the truth which is taught by the Church, since the challenge of the age was to defend the truth from false prophets who came as wolves in lamb's clothing.

Mendicant Friars

Both Dominic, and Francis his contemporary, were compelled by the love of God not to be confined to the monastic way of life. They developed a style which came to be called mendicant,[45] whereby friars could take their cell with them in their hearts due to the exigency of preaching the gospel. In the thirteenth century there was a dearth of good preaching in the Church since the local priests, poorly trained, were mainly sacramentally focussed and preaching was seen as the preserve of bishops. But the bishops were mainly feudal lords, preoccupied with administration of property and gaining taxes from their dependents. Few were dedicated preachers. This was a time when the feudal system was breaking down and was being replaced by local communes. Consequently, often the bishops were out of touch with the people. Under these conditions many sects sprouted, often anti-clerical, and peddling a counterfeit gospel.

This popular preaching movement was hugely problematic for the Church authorities. It says much for Pope Innocent III that he recognised in both Francis and Dominic an antidote to the problem by allowing to be unleashed in the Church two new congregations of authentic popular gospel preachers.

The Dispersion

By 1217 Dominic had gathered about 30 men at Toulouse, but they were not to be together for long. On the feast of the Assumption Dominic declared to the brothers that they were to be sent out in small groups throughout the world. Until then they were simply focussed on the region of the south of France, winning people back to the Catholic faith. Now to their surprise their leader "lifted the lid" way beyond their expectations. This was something they did not foresee. By the grace of God, and because they trusted Dominic's holiness, they submitted to this wild project. They were to be dispersed to cities and lands unknown to them. When some naturally protested the wisdom of such a move Dominic was to say, "Do not oppose me, for I know that the seed will go mouldy and rot if it is hoarded up; it will be fruitful if it is sown widely."[46] Four were sent to Spain, seven in two groups to Paris. These were the most solid and intellectually capable brothers, who would serve in universities. A few friars were sent to Orleans and others to Bologna. Some local born friars remained in Toulouse, including Dominic's first two companions, Peter Seila and his brother Thomas. Dominic then returned to Rome, and through his friend Cardinal Ugolino, who had also been a great supporter of Francis, he had the Order recommended to all the bishops by means of a Papal bull.

The extraordinary missionary zeal of Dominic was no more evident than when he courageously flung his neophyte preachers beyond the security of St Romain to the ends of the earth. No doubt he was inspired by the words of Jesus at the end of Matthew's gospel which he knew by heart: "Go, therefore, make disciples of all the nations, baptising them in the name of the Father, Son and Holy Spirit and teaching them all I have commanded. And remember I am with you to the end of the age" (Mt 28:19). Dominic expected his brothers to devote themselves entirely to the work of evangelisation. Prepared in silence, prayer and study they were to be men of action making the preaching of the Good News their life's work in thorough-going service (cf. 2 Tim 4:5).

Bold Expansion

With this courageous dispersion Dominic's mission became a universal outreach. One of the most daring ventures was the way the Polish mission opened.[47] The bishop of Cracow was in Rome on pilgrimage with two of his nephews, who were brothers, and canons of the Cathedral of Crakow. They had been present when Dominic through prayer had raised a bishop's nephew from the dead at St Sixtus Church. Not surprisingly the pilgrims were deeply impressed. Ivo, the bishop of Cracow had been begging Dominic to send missionaries to Poland. The problem was that no brothers spoke Polish and it was difficult to equip anyone in the language. So Dominic came up with the perfect solution: the two nephews, who were devout young canons, could become Dominicans and lead the mission! They already knew the language so that would solve the problem! After a couple of days of reflection the two nephews, Hyacinth and Ceslaus, presented themselves to receive the habit of the Order. Together with two other candidates Dominic took them into six months training himself at Santa Sabina, the Rome headquarters of the Order.

It was an amazingly fruitful novitiate birthing an ardent

missionary zeal. Ceslaus worked in Bohemia on the fringe of Tartary, Hyacinth travelled through Russia, Sweden, Norway, Prussia and into Asia. He is recorded as travelling more than twenty-five thousand miles on foot in proclaiming the gospel. The extreme risks Dominic and his brothers took were an expression of their deep faith in the Lord's promise that, whenever we go forth to preach the gospel, God will be with us. In their novitiate they tapped into the heart of God for the lost and were unstoppable in their zeal for the salvation of souls. They were formed in two fundamental charisms which sum up the primary focus of the priestly apostolate in any age: "prayer and the service of the word" (Acts 6:4).

The Gift of Prayer

Dominic's contemporaries testify that his way of praying was simple, ardent and varied. At one time he would be spontaneously thanking and praising God with his lips, and at another quietly contemplative and rapt in love of the Lord. While his brothers cannot describe to us his interior experience, they give graphic descriptions of his various bodily postures in prayer, and the aspiration behind each of them. He loved to pray bowing before the altar which is a symbol of Christ present or before a crucifix so that "Christ, who was so greatly humbled for us, should see us humbled before his exaltation".[48] He sometimes prayed prostrated with his face on the ground crying out to the Lord for mercy (cf Luke 18:13). This posture evoked in him the grace of compunction, weeping before the Lord for his sins. Occasionally Dominic was observed to pray by alternately kneeling and then standing before the crucifix. He would kneel out of sorrow for his sins, and then stand in the assurance of God's mercy, full of radiant joy, and "like a thirsty man coming to a spring of water" his prayer would become more insistent and his movements more passionate. Another characteristic posture was to pray standing unsupported with his hands open, as if he were holding an open book, conversing intimately with the Lord, and then he would maybe join his hands in reverence, and then maybe stretch his arms out in prayer like the priest at Mass. Each of these postures expressed the changing movements of the Spirit within him as he communed with the Lord.

Another posture that Dominic liked was to stand before the crucifix with his arms outstretched as far as they could go, joining with Jesus' prayer as he was stretched out on the Cross for our sake. He loved to recite the psalm, "I call to you, Lord, all day long; to you I stretch out my hands" (Psalm 88:10). Another expressive gesture in prayer was to stretch his whole body up towards heaven, "like an arrow being shot straight up in the air: his hands were stretched right up above his head, either held together or open as if to receive something from heaven".[49] He would often be on the tip of his toes as he reached upward with intense desire for God. He was not able to hold that position for long, but, caught up in rapture, it was like a dart of love rising through any darkness, inspired by a deep infusion of the interior gifts of the Holy Spirit. At other times Dominic would pray with the Scripture or some other spiritual book, "letting the sweetness of what he read touch his mind", and then responding with all his heart. This was the "*lectio divina*" which was the traditional way that the monks pondered scripture texts, chewing over the words and letting the power of the word of God open their hearts in love. The final way of prayer was when Dominic was travelling by foot from one town to the next on his preaching expeditions. He would either go ahead a little from the others, or drop behind so he could be alone. He would use the time to hold in his heart a scripture text upon which he had been meditating. The fire of love would be enkindled within him constantly as he held the word of God within him and let the light of the Holy Spirit bring wisdom and understanding to him. This was the secret of his intimacy with Jesus, and of his powerful preaching and his courage in the face of adversity.

Preaching: An Ecclesial Grace

At the time of Dominic many lay movements had arisen with itinerant preachers, claiming the charismatic gift of preaching but without an ecclesiastical mandate. The so-called "Poor Men of Lyons", or Waldensians, founded by Peter Waldes, a merchant of Lyons (+1218) was an example of this independent preaching ministry. They lived a penitential way of life embracing a radical evangelical poverty. Innocent III had welcomed them and authorised them to give moral exhortations to the people, but they could preach on the gospels only with express permission from the bishop. Unfortunately they eventually turned anti-clerical, claiming the authority of the bible over the Pope. They taught that confession to a holy layman was better than confessing to a sinful priest, and rejected popular devotions, which unfortunately were largely lining the pockets of the clergy. Not surprisingly the Church was finding it difficult to regulate the gift of preaching.

Unfortunately these lay movements did not gain the traction in the Church they needed, and the new evangelical energy they promised was largely wasted. This was partly due to their excessively misdirected enthusiasm, and refusal to submit humbly to proper authority, but also partly because the clericalised Church of the time could not find a way to accommodate them. Whatever we might say about the failure of the Church to support the voice of the laity calling for reform, we can affirm strongly that no new movement in the Church can be truly authentic unless it is humbly submitted to Church authority. As we have seen, Dominic was successful in winning approbation from the Church hierarchy, who were convinced not only of his holiness, but also of his theological and exegetical competence as a priest, and were impressed by his effectiveness in combatting heresy.

Dominic always understood the gift of preaching as an ecclesial grace. It was a charism within the Church to be exercised for the edification of the members of the Church and as part of the Church's mission for the salvation of souls. Dominic began his preaching career under Bishop Diego, who within himself combined both the charismatic gift and hierarchical authority. Dominic never moved outside of submission to Church authority. He was acutely aware that his preaching ministry only found its legitimacy within and for the Church. He never saw the grace of preaching to be over against the institutional Church, rather it was an "institutional charism". The grace of preaching springs up from the heart of the Church by the action of the Holy Spirit. It is the very essence of the Church to evangelize, and the preaching ministry is a core activity in this essential mission. The Church is birthed again and again by Spirit-filled preaching. The Church is built up by preaching. By charismatic preaching divine life flows in, through and for the Church.

Preaching: a Charism

The charism of preaching is a supernatural gift that goes beyond one's natural talents, knowledge or skills. It is not so much about personal magnetism or oratorical gifts. It is rather the gift of utterance which Peter experienced on the day of Pentecost. It is a gift of the Holy Spirit whereby the word of God is proclaimed in such a clear and convincing way that hearts are opened and conversion occurs. It is not a trade to be learned through techniques, not even an art to be mastered. It is a gift. The Holy Spirit gives fire to the preacher by filling the soul with divine love. The Spirit enlightens the preacher with understanding of the mysteries to be proclaimed. The Spirit grants wisdom to know how to speak and what to say to any particular group of people. The Spirit provides the words that are most apt for the listeners at that time. Jesus promised:

> You will be dragged before governors and kings for my sake, to bear witness before them to the pagans. But when they hand you over, do not worry about how to speak or what to say; what you are to say will be given to you when the time comes; because it is not you who will be speaking; the Spirit of your Father will be speaking in you. (Matthew 10:18-20)

The charism of preaching means that the word spoken will ignite a fire in the heart of listeners, convincing them of the truth proclaimed and stirring them to repentance and faith. This is what happened at Pentecost, when at the end of Peter's charismatic preaching, the people cried out "What must we do, brothers?" They were impelled to respond. Charismatic preaching will always seek a response appropriate to the message since "the word of God is something alive and active: it cuts like any double-edged sword but more finely...and lays bare the secret thoughts of men" (Heb 4:12). The word of God, *dabar* in the Hebrew, is not empty sounds without having any effect, nor is it pleasing tones that tickle ears but bring no change. It is an event; things happen when the word is preached. Preaching with the Spirit and fire is guaranteed to stir up conversion. The word of God which is preached in the Spirit will open the hearts of the listeners. When Paul proclaimed the word to Lydia by the river outside the gates of Philippi we are told, "she listened to us, and the Lord opened her heart to accept what Paul was saying" (Acts 16:14). She immediately asked for baptism.

Dominic and Francis

While it may not be substantiated as historically accurate, there is a strong tradition that Dominic and Francis of Assisi met while they were both at the Fourth Lateran Council called by Pope Innocent III. Probably the meeting took place in the home of Cardinal Hugolin who, as a trusted adviser to the Pope, had been an enthusiastic supporter of both the Franciscan and Dominican movements. One can only imagine what words would have passed between them, but we can be sure there was mutual encouragement and kinship of spirit. Their common heart for the Church's mission of proclaiming the Good News was the most powerful influence for renewal in the Church of their time. There's no point in comparing the missionary gift each brought to the Church. Rather it is for us to pray that the Holy Spirit in our day will inspire the gift of preaching in a fresh and new way, so that fire will come to the earth.

CATHERINE OF SIENA

Chronology

1347 - born in Siena

1365 - enters into solitude

1368 - called out of solitude to serve the poor

1374 - begins her public activity in Florence

1377 - succeeds in persuading the Pope to return to Rome

1378 - dictates the *Dialogue*

1380 - dies in Rome on April 29

Quotes

You, eternal Trinity, are a deep sea.

The more I enter you,

the more I discover,

and the more I discover,

the more I seek you.

God is more willing to pardon

than we have been to sin.

In your nature, eternal Godhead,

I shall come to know my nature

and what is my nature, boundless love?

It is fire,

because you are nothing but a fire of love.

Be who God meant you to be
and you will set the world on fire.

CATHERINE OF SIENA

Catherine Benincasa was born in Siena on 25 March 1347. She was the fourteenth child of her parents Jacopo and Lapa, who had already lost nine others at child birth. Being the youngest she was loved dearly by her parents. At the age of six, already very devout, Catherine experienced a vision of Jesus filling her soul with intense love. Growing into teenage years her family were already preparing for her betrothal. But she resisted vigorously all of their attempts to guide her in this direction, secretly consecrating herself to the Lord as a virgin. At the age of fifteen the issue came to a head and she sought the advice of a Dominican priest, who advised cropping off her hair as a sign to her parents that her life was given to God. To the dismay of her parents she did so immediately.

The Journey Inwards

The family home in Siena was in the shadow of the Church of St Dominic. This was the church in which she prayed, received the sacraments and listened to sermons. She imbibed the Dominican spirit, falling in love with Dominic, who she described later as "an apostle in the world" who sowed God's word wherever he went, "dispelling darkness and giving light".[50] She was drawn to join the Mantellate (the Cloaked Sisters), a lay movement of holy women living out the Dominican spirit of prayer, penance and the apostolate. After a prolonged battle with her parents, at the age of eighteen she received the Dominican habit of the Mantellate. This marked the beginning of three years in solitude within her bedroom in the family home. She only emerged from seclusion to attend morning Mass each day. During this time in the desert Catherine allowed herself to be claimed by the Lord as his own. She discovered the God who was insanely in love with her, and found herself in return madly in love with him. Later in the *Dialogue* she voices it this way:

O eternal Father! O fiery abyss of love! O eternal beauty, O eternal wisdom, O eternal goodness, O eternal mercy! O hope and refuge of sinners! O immeasurable generosity! O eternal, infinite Good! O mad lover! And you have no need of your creature? It seems so to me, for you act as if you could not live without her, in spite of the fact that you are Life itself, and everything has life from you and nothing can have life without you. Why then are you so mad? Because you have fallen in love with what you have made! You are pleased and delighted over her within yourself, as if you were drunk with desire for her salvation. She runs away from you and you go looking for her. She strays and you draw closer to her. You clothed yourself in our humanity, and nearer than that you could not have come. And what shall I say? What shall I stutter, 'A-a' because there is nothing else I know how to say. Finite language cannot express the emotion of the soul who longs for you infinitely.[51]

Unquenchable Fire

There was a divine fire burning within Catherine that could not be extinguished. As we read in the Song of Songs, "Love is a flash of fire from the heart of God that no torrents can quench and no floods drown. For love someone is willing to give up all that they have and count nothing of the cost" (Song 8:6). This fire had penetrated to the core of Catherine's being. She sings of this in one of her prayers:

In your nature, eternal Godhead,

I shall come to know my nature.

And what is my nature, boundless love?

It is fire,

Because you are nothing but a fire of love.

And you have given humankind

A share in this nature

For by the fire of love you created us.

And so with all other people

And every created thing;

You made them out of love.[52]

We don't have a lot of detail about this time of solitude which formed Catherine for her later intense engagement in the world. But we know that, although she was unschooled as was the custom for women in those days, she begged the Lord to be able read and was graciously bestowed with the gift from on high.

We know also that towards the end of these three years she was beset with terrible temptations to give up her life of prayer and penance, taunting her that she will not have the power to persevere. Worse still she was deluged with sensual thoughts, horrible visions and delusions. In all of this darkness that persisted for a long time the previous sweetness of the Lord's presence disappeared and she was left in a void. Yet she didn't succumb to the suggestions of the evil one, but pressed on even harder without consolation. She would pray in dark faith in words that felt hollow, "I rely on the Lord Jesus Christ and not on myself", repeating these words over and over again. Finally, the light of the Lord's love broke into her soul again, and she was filled with the experience of his love. She cried out to the Lord. "Where were you when my heart was filled with the agony of all these horrors?" The Lord answered her, "Was it not I myself, hidden in your heart's core? It was I who was working in you all this time. Hidden in your heart, I was guarding it from your enemies on every side".[53] When instructing her companions later she drew upon this experience to illustrate never to give up prayer in times of discouragement, and that times of trial increase our dependence on God alone.

Catherine's seclusion came to its completion at the age of twenty with her experience of a "mystical marriage" with the Lord in which she was presented to Jesus by Mary and given a ring on her finger which only she could see. She was to begin taking meals with her family again and move into the world under the direction of the Spirit. At first Catherine was dismayed by this command and protested. She was reluctant to leave her solitude since she was afraid of losing her intimacy with the Lord. In prayer she told the Lord of her fears, and received an encouraging answer:

> I have no intention whatever of parting you from myself, but rather of making sure to bind you to me all the closer by the bond of love for your neighbour. Remember that I have laid down two commandments of love: love of me and love of your neighbour...It is the righteousness of these two commandments that I want you to fulfil. On two feet you must walk my way.[54]

Two Wings of Love

Now returning to the world Catherine was to walk on two feet, not only one. She was to keep the love of God and love of neighbour inseparable. If one increases so does the other. If one decreases so does the other. Another image Catherine received was the "two wings of love". Just as a bird cannot fly without two wings so the true follower of Jesus must fly with both love of God and love of neighbour. In the next three years Catherine threw herself into charitable works near her home, attending to the needs of the sick and the poor. But she still preferred her solitude and carried some reluctance in her heart towards throwing herself into caring for others. As one of the Mantellate, she ministered to those who no one else would touch; the leprous Tecca, the abusive Palmerina, the dying Andrea, who, even though suffering from sores all over her body, spread slanderous rumours about Catherine who was tending to her wounds.

Catherine would picture the wounded Jesus in this miserable soul, Andrea. One day when caring for her Catherine was so full of revulsion for this despicable woman that she forced herself to drink the putrid water in which she had washed Andrea's sores[55]. Miraculously Catherine's disgust turned to joy as she found herself mystically drinking the blood of Jesus. This led to her offering her heart to Jesus in return for his heart of unbounded love being given to her. She now had the Lord's heart for others. She confided to Raymond of Capua, her spiritual director, that with this revelation and its new empowerment she was no longer the same person. She had an inner fire within her giving her boundless love for others and endless zeal to work for their salvation.[56] She heard the Lord say to her, "Those who want to gain lose, and those who are willing to lose gain. Those who are willing to lose their own consolation for their neighbour's welfare receive and gain me and their neighbours, if they help and serve them lovingly. And so they enjoy the graciousness of my charity at all times".[57]

An Intercessory Heart

This new awareness of loving one's neighbour gave Catherine a large heart for the world, an intercessory heart. She considered that anyone who is drawn into the heart of Jesus will have a heart which pleads the mercy of God for others. Intercession is not an optional devotion, but flows from union with the heart of God. The Father himself asks us to intercede for the lost. Love teaches us to knock on the door of God's heart unceasingly. When we bind ourselves to Jesus' intercession for the world we unite ourselves to those for whom we intercede. They may be incapable of making a yes to God with their lives, but we can do so for them, standing in their place before God, and drawing from the heart of God his boundless mercy upon them. God the Father places in our hearts a deep love for others, especially those he has given to our care, and when we pray for them our prayer will be answered.

Catherine urges us to unite our prayer with that of Christ who continues to pray for us all, pouring out the same blood that was won for our salvation. In Hebrews we read, "It follows then that his power to save is utterly certain, since he is living forever to intercede for all who come to God through him" (Heb 7:25). She knew that God's salvation won for us by Jesus crucified must be accepted by human freedom. We must say yes to what has been done for us. She says to the Lord, "Though you created us without our help, it is not your will to save us without our help".[58] But so many in the world are locked in selfishness and fear, unable to make their yes to God's love. Hence the need for intercession. Having discovered the inseparability of the "two wings of love", love of God and love of neighbour, Catherine could see with a new clarity that the further she went in union with God the more she was drawn into service and intercession for others. God could have healed the world without our help, but he has so respected our free will that he waits upon our intercession.

As she was drawn more into the heart of Jesus in contemplation she found herself having a fire of compassion for others. We cannot repay God for his unselfish love, but this gift impels us to love others. She began to feel the fire of God's love for others, and that the power of intercessory prayer surpasses anything else we can do for God. We are to feed the flame of our desire to see people brought back to the living God, and to let "not a moment pass without crying out" for others.[59] The more we abandon ourselves to the Lord the more we find his heart and are joined with his "hungry desire for the salvation of souls".[60] We are joined with Jesus crucified as he cried out "I thirst", and seek to satiate his thirst for souls.

Interceding in Weakness

Catherine images the heart of those resistant to the will of God to be as hard as a diamond, which can only be broken open by the power of the blood of Jesus. In intercession we are to stand at the foot of the Cross of Jesus and collect the blood poured out for all and then cast it upon the hard-hearted for their conversion. Only the blood of Jesus continually poured out upon the world through intercessory prayer will soften the resistance to the gospel message. We need not be worried about our own weakness and sinfulness as if this will diminish our effectiveness as intercessors. To the contrary far from obstructing the power of our intercessory prayer, our weakness and sinfulness will attract the mercy of God to come upon us and those for whom we pray. She says to the Lord, "No matter where I turn I find nothing but your mercy. This is why I run crying to your mercy to have mercy on the world"[61] Catherine calls for more people to become "christs" for the Church. "O best of remedy givers! Give us then these 'christs', who will live in continual watching and tears and prayers for the world's salvation".[62]

Now that Catherine was in the active apostolate the gift of preaching began to be manifest. Raymond tells us that her "charismatic utterance" burst forth in words that "burnt like a torch". All who came to her were touched and moved by her words. Even those who came to argue with her or to belittle her would inevitably "leave her presence in tears".[63] People would flock to her because she did not speak with the language of learning but with fire of the Holy Spirit. While at times she preached to large congregations, she preferred to meet people in small gatherings. No matter what the circumstances were, her words invariably opened up hearts because of the anointing of the Holy Spirit upon her.

Contemplation

When Catherine left her private room, which had been like a monastic cell, to face the world the Lord helped her see that he had given her an inner cell within her heart. In the midst of extraordinarily busy activity and public ministry she learnt to make a cell within her heart which she would never have to leave. However, living within this inner dwelling place did not mean an escape from the world. Rather, she found within herself the fire of God's love in such a way that it drew her into his loving arms and at the same time into the embrace of others. It is within this "holy abyss" that we come to know God and ourselves. From within this place there is a fountain of living water, the Holy Spirit, rising and expanding the heart to the love of God and the love of neighbour. This realisation was the foundation of Catherine's spirituality, and undoubtedly is a crucial part of her spiritual legacy which we can draw upon today.

Raymond of Capua tells us that during her time of solitude Catherine received a revelation from the Lord which shaped her whole spiritual outlook. The Lord said to her, "Do you know, daughter, who you are and who I am? If you know these two things you have beatitude in your grasp. You are she who is not, and I AM WHO IS". If she let this truth fill her whole being she was assured she would find every blessing.[64] As we dwell upon the goodness and mercy of God and allow the light of the Spirit to show us the truth about ourselves we discover a two-fold self-knowledge. Catherine calls us to gaze into the "gentle mirror of God". It is a liberating experience to behold oneself as God beholds me, no more, no less. I will find my identity in God and nowhere else; I find who I am by surrendering myself to the great I AM.

Firstly, we become aware of our inherent dignity and goodness given by our Creator who loved us into being and made us in his image and likeness. Created for God we participate in his beauty, redeemed by the precious blood of Jesus we are children of God, heirs of the kingdom, with immeasurable worth in God's eyes, destined for fullness of life with God forever. She hears God saying to her:

> It was with providence that I created you, and when I contemplated my creature in myself I fell in love with the beauty of my creation…All this my gentle providence did, only that you might be capable of understanding and enjoying me and rejoicing in my goodness by seeing me eternally.[65]

Secondly we discover our weakness, brokenness and proneness to sin. This is not a morbid exercise in introspection or psychological analysis. Rather it is gentle revelation from our loving Father which helps us see our utter need for his mercy and our total need for Jesus as our redeemer. It is seeing ourselves through God's eyes. He shows us our nothingness. Jesus told us "cut off from me you can do nothing" (John 15:5). We realise our utter need for him, not only to keep our heart beating and our lungs breathing, but also to be able to overcome sin and temptation, to break the power of the flesh, and to resist temptations. We discover that any virtue gained is only because of his mercy. In the depths of the heart there is a perversity that would swamp us if it were not for God's mercy. It is such a liberating revelation to see the "slum condition" of my soul, but to know my sure hope is with my Saviour. Earlier I related how the Lord had allowed Catherine to experience the darkness of faith and terrifying temptations, so that she would appreciate her total dependence upon him. It takes a long journey for us to admit in the depth of the soul our absolute need for God; that our life and everything we have comes from his mercy.

While knowing our nothingness we must also know the other part: "I am the One who is!" This reminds us of Moses before the burning bush. Having taken off his shoes as a sign of surrender to the Almighty God, he now receives the answer to his question, "I am who I am" (Ex3:14). This was not an ontological statement about the inner being of God. It would best be translated, "I am the God who is *with you*", the God of Abraham, Isaac, and Jacob, the God who acts in our history with redeeming love and power. Jesus is the fulfilment of this revelation. In John's gospel the many "I am" statements identify Jesus with the God of the Exodus, and powerfully express his saving power in our midst: "I am the Way the Truth and the Life", "I am the light of the world", "I am the bread of life", and "I am the good Shepherd". Without his redeeming love we would be eternally lost, and without his mercy we would fall into the abyss of sin. Knowing our utter neediness and fragility, we can place all our trust in his mercy. With this perspective we are not afraid of our weaknesses and brokenness, since our weakness draws the power of Christ to us. God's power is manifest best in weakness. Paul heard the Lord say to him, "My grace is enough for you, my power is at its best in weakness" (2Cor 12:9).

Catherine urged her companions to hold both truths together, knowledge of self and knowledge of God. If we know only about our broken human condition we are liable to fall into despair. Knowing ourselves outside of God leaves us confused and discouraged by our weakness. On the other hand if we know only about God's goodness and have no insight into our brokenness and inner poverty we may well fall into pride and presumption. The "gentle mirror" of God will open up for us this double revelation. Catherine counsels us not to be thrown when inner struggles occur, either temptations, or times of desolation or aridity. These are not times to escape from the cell and allow our flesh desires to take us away from living in God.

She remembers her own time of testing and how at the end of it the Lord showed her he had not abandoned her but was dwelling with her at the core of her being, otherwise she would not have endured. By staying faithful to the inner cell in these times of interior or exterior struggles, we grow in surrender to God's will, and discover for ourselves that in God light is born out of darkness and strength out of weakness. She reminds us that God hones out virtue in the heart by allowing us to endure temptations to the contrary. For example he allows sensual temptations so that in resisting them by his grace we are strengthened in purity of heart. All of this is geared towards us really becoming who we are meant to be in God. And when we fully realise ourselves in God, then our impact on the world will be immense. Catherine's short life was a living example of this. As her most famous quote puts it:

"Be who God meant you to be, and you will set the world on fire".[66]

The Way of Christ Crucified

In one of her letters Catherine sums up her way to God, "The way has been made. It is the doctrine of Christ crucified. Whoever walks along this way.....reaches the most perfect light".[67] Her whole spirituality was focussed on Jesus crucified. If we gaze upon him and allow his redeeming love to dwell in our hearts we shall ultimately become like him. She had a profound appreciation of the mercy of God revealed through Jesus' death on the Cross, and in particular in the shedding of his blood. In the Cross of Jesus Catherine found the magnetic power of God's love drawing her close to him. She says that no human power held him to the cross. He was bound by nails, but that was his self-offering because of our sin. The only power that held him fast was the power of love.[68] "He bows his head to greet you, wears the crown of thorns to adorn you, stretches out his arms to embrace you, lets his feet be nailed that he may stand with you".[69]

Lifted up on the Cross for our sake Jesus in his suffering radiates immense, unconditional love as he gave himself completely for our sake. Catherine focussed her loving attention upon the heart of Jesus pierced by the lance from which flowed blood and water. She saw this as the ultimate sign of the infinite love of God for us. In the piercing of his side Jesus reveals for us his heart broken open in love for the world. Catherine heard him say, "I wanted you to see my inmost heart, so that you would see that I loved you more than finite suffering could show".[70] While the physical sufferings of Jesus move us, this still may not be enough for us to really know the infinite love he has for us. We need revelation on high to see the boundless love of God contained in the human heart of Jesus as he gave himself up for us. Catherine saw the blood pouring out of the side of Christ until there was no more as a definitive sign of the truth of God's mercy towards us. He shed the last drop of his blood, and this has rendered infinite mercy visible. Looking upon the Cross we see our capacity for hatred and destruction; but we see even more so his infinite capacity for mercy and forgiveness.

The blood of Jesus purifies us of all sins (1Jn 1:7). It cleanses us of our defilement. Catherine writes in one of her letters that Jesus will wash us in his blood, bathe us in forgiveness, and hide us in the cavern of his side.[71] There in his side we can find refuge, a hiding place from the forces that may seek to destroy us. The blood of Jesus was the ransom paid for our sins, "Remember the ransom that was paid to free you from the futile way of life of your ancestors handed down was not paid in anything corruptible, neither in silver nor gold, but in the precious blood of a lamb without spot or stain, namely Christ" (1 Pet 1:18-19). As such it is a sign of God's infinite mercy which we could not have merited or gained by anything we have done. His mercy is sheer gift from God. "But God loved us with so much love that he was rich in mercy: when we were dead through our sins, he brought us to life with Christ…it is through grace that you have been saved, through faith; not by anything of your own, but by a gift from God" (Eph 2: 4-8).

The Power of the Blood of Jesus

Catherine was thoroughly convinced of the mercy of God for every human person. Even someone at the moment of death, who has lived a sinful life, has only to turn to the Father of mercy and trust in him. The voice of the Lord had convinced her: "No one ought to despair. No, reach out trustingly for the blood, no matter what sins you have committed, for my mercy, which you receive in the blood, is incomparably greater than all the sins that have ever been committed in the world".[72]

She says that despair rejects God's mercy and is greater than any sin. She heard the Lord say, "The despair of Judas displeased me more and was a greater insult to my Son than his betrayal had been". At death guilt can assail us but we need to surrender in trust into the arms of God's mercy. She encourages her friends, "Hide yourself under the wings of the mercy of God, for he is more inclined to pardon than you are to sin. Bathe yourself in the blood of Christ".[73]

Wounded and broken as we are, damaged by our sin and the sin of others against us, we so much need to confidently cry out to God for mercy. He shed his blood for our healing. Catherine urges us to bathe our entire being in the blood of Jesus which brings cleansing and healing. Often there is a stubbornness of heart which resists God's grace and can make us hard of heart towards others and not willing to forgive offences that have been made against us. Catherine says the answer is in the blood of Jesus. Come to the foot of the Cross as Mary Magdalene did and be bathed in his blood. This has power to open the heart in love and forgiveness. The blood of Jesus alone can "shatter the diamond" hardness of our hearts. She says that even if we have spent our entire life in sin we must cry out with Mary Magdalen for the mercy which God is so ready to give. His mercy is infinitely more powerful than sin. She says, "I will hide myself in his blood, and so my wickedness will be consumed".[74]

Catherine's confidence in the power of the blood of Jesus has no bounds. We are to soak our whole selves in his blood, allowing our minds to be cleansed at the conscious, semi-conscious and unconscious levels. In intercession we are to plead the blood of Jesus on all those who do not know the love of God, especially those trapped in overtly sinful lives. The power of his blood alone will break open their hearts to love. We may feel we or others are not good enough, not worthy enough to come into the presence of God. But "through the blood of Jesus we have the right to enter the sanctuary" (Heb 10:19). By the shedding of his blood Jesus has opened our way into the holiness of God. We can confidently enter the sanctuary of our hearts and find him there to embrace us with his merciful love. While we were not worthy, he has made us worthy.

For Catherine the blood of Jesus is also an invitation for us to mingle our blood with his in self-giving service in preaching the gospel and, if necessary, martyrdom. Her love for the blood of Jesus stirred her to desire union with him by shedding her own blood for his sake. As Jesus has paid the ultimate price for us, we also should be prepared to pay the ultimate price for him and for his Church's mission. She wanted to be with those who have "washed their robes white again in the blood of the Lamb" (Rev 7:14). Once in Florence when Catherine, on a peace-making mission, was falsely accused of inciting a riot, an angry mob broke into the garden of the home where she was staying. They were intent on murdering her. As the would-be assassin drew near to Catherine, she was so full of joy and courage in anticipation of her martyrdom that the man became confused, lost heart for the task, and fled. Catherine was left weeping that her dream had been denied her.

Providence of God

On her death bed Catherine confided in her friends that her only task her whole life long had been to hold on with unshakeable hope and trust in the providence of God. Our resources are so frail, but God has absolute power over everything. We either choose to trust in God for everything or we fall into despair. As Jesus said, "If the smallest things are outside your control, why worry about the rest?" (Lk 12:26). God is a loving Father who knows our every need. "Set your hearts on his kingdom and these other things will be given you as well". (Lk 12:31). We are not to trust in our own resources, but to have radical trust in the providence of God. We must acknowledge our helplessness and beg God's help. "Cast all of your anxieties on the Lord, for he cares for you" (1Pet 5:7). The whole universe is ruled by the provident mercy of God. Madly in love with us, he wants only our good. If we trust in his providence we will not only know his care for us in a theoretical way but through practical experience.

Catherine wants us to know that even in life's tragedies God's providence can bring good. As Paul says, "All things work towards the good for those who love the Lord" (Rom 8:28). God permits, what she calls, the "wearisome thorns" of life out of love for us so that we painfully learn over the years that nothing created can be a god for us. He allows our false supports and investments to be stripped away, so that we are free to love him above all things. The Lord instructed Catherine, "I wanted her to learn that although everyone else may fail her, I, her Creator, would never fail her". No matter how distressing a situation may become there is a hidden gift, "a wealth hidden within". No matter how terrible a calamity may occur it can always be turned into a font of grace.[75] After all, the greatest tragedy of humanity was when the innocent Son of God was slammed against a cross on Calvary. Yet from this tragedy flowed the enormous grace of the salvation of the human race. No matter what the cross that comes to us, because of Jesus, it can be a source of life and strength for us and others.

Catherine suggests that in one's life-journey the Lord often provides "tricks of providence", events and circumstances that we could not have expected, which in some way serve to burst our bubble of vanity and humble us. We may have sought affection in something or someone, or set our sights on a prestigious goal, or given our unbridled energies towards a beloved project, and find it all crumbles before us, and there is nothing to boast about. These struggles that humble us are God's own gift to us. She says, "The soul comes to perfection by fighting these battles, because there she *experiences* my divine providence, whereas before this she only believed in it".[76] Paul was left with the "thorn in the flesh" to humble him, so that he would rely more fully on the power of God's love. We find this sort of "pricking" happens in life so that we grow in humility and become more compassionate to others. The Lord wants us to practically experience the truth of our own weakness so that we will become merciful towards others.[77]

A Hidden Grace

For personal healing of all the wounds in our life the Lord will often apply bitter remedies. She points out that usually the medicine that tastes the worst is the best for the body's health. So it is with the soul. Like an unpleasant medicine that brings healing, God's love can transform tragedies into something that is sweet and full of love. With Augustine she pronounces that God who is all good would not allow evil to happen to us if he did not intend to bring a greater good from it. He brings life out of chaos. She uses the image of an orange which has a bitter rind on the outside but inside is delightfully sweet. Calamities and experiences of loss in life can be like that. Beneath the external bitterness we can by God's grace find a hidden sweetness.[78]

At a certain point Catherine heard the Lord say to her, "Think of me and I will think of you" – that is, not to think of herself and her weaknesses and inadequacies; not to think of how much she lacks in resources for dealing with life's problems. Rather she is to focus on God, his goodness, power and mercy. She is to give herself to God in every situation, no matter how desperate it may seem. If we "think of him" in any time of physical and spiritual need there is no longer any reason for anxiety. Rather than be preoccupied by our own needs, our own brokenness and inadequacy, we are to attend to his love and mercy. Rather than becoming anxious about our lack, we need to look in faith to the Lord who is all sufficient in fulfilling our needs.

> Why must you have such care for yourselves? Let God's providence watch over you. His eyes are on you continually in your fears. Not a moment passes but he is thinking of your welfare.[79]

She heard the Lord encouraging her: "So consider it useless to wear yourself out guarding your city unless it is guarded by me. Every effort is useless for those who think they can guard their city by their own toil or concern, for I alone am the guardian".[80] As the psalmist prays, "If the Lord does not build the house, in vain do its builders labour; if the Lord does not watch over the city, in vain does the watchman keep vigil. In vain is their earlier rising, your going later to rest..." (Psalm 127:1-2).

Failure and Defeat, but Victory in the Lord

During her life, and especially at her death, Catherine's trust in providence was tested to the limit. She died in Rome at the age of thirty three years. From the time when at the age of twenty one she emerged from her three years of seclusion she had only another twelve years to live. She packed more into this extraordinary time of apostolic activity than most who live to ninety years of age. All of this as a young woman in a society where women usually did not have a voice! In a church in Pisa she experienced a mystical union with the Cross of Jesus, by which she received an invisible stigmata. After this she always experienced the pain of the wounds of Jesus, but without the visible signs on her body. This experience gave a new fire to her preaching ministry. A woman of her times, she zealously preached a Crusade to the Holy Land throughout the cities of Italy. As a peace-maker she worked hard to mediate a political rift between the city of Florence and the Pope, which at one stage led to Florence being placed under an interdict by the Pope, forbidding them to celebrate sacraments. Then with indomitable courage she invited herself to the Papal Palace at Avignon, where Pope Gregory VII resided, to persuade him that he should return the Papacy to Rome where it belonged. He finally conceded to this fiery young woman who spoke the truth from her heart. But, unfortunately, this victory backfired. When Gregory, finally ensconced in Rome, died, Urban VI was elected, but he soon turned out to be a tyrant despised by all. The French Cardinals and others opposed Urban's election, on the dubious grounds that they had been pressured by the Italian populace. So they elected another Pope! The Church which Catherine loved was now bitterly divided.

On her deathbed Catherine was filled with disappointment, but refused to despair. She blamed herself for pressuring Pope Gregory to come to Rome, which had sparked the rebellion of the French

Cardinals against his successor. Having worked tirelessly for Church reform she now found herself defending Pope Urban who was legitimately elected, but had become tyrannical and was hated by all. She had failed to mediate peace between Florence and the Papacy, even though the two parties had eventually honed out an agreement without her. On top of this she was heart-broken that her life-long friend and spiritual director, Raymond of Capua, had in her eyes cowardly refused to risk martyrdom by fulfilling his commission to preach to the King of France. To add to her woes the disciples she left behind in Siena when she was summonsed to Rome by the Pope had disbanded only a couple of months after her departure. Even though she had friends around her when she died, she could not escape a profound sense of personal failure. She died heart-broken for the Church which she loved so dearly but felt helpless to reform. In her final words she placed herself unreservedly in the hands of her Beloved, and called upon the mercy of the blood of Jesus to save her.

IGNATIUS LOYOLA

Chronology

1491 - born at Loyola Castle, Spain

1521 - wounded in battle; recuperates in Loyola Castle

1522 - Manresa retreat

1523 - pilgrimage to Jerusalem

1528 - arrives in Paris

1534 - Vows at Montmartre

1537 - arrives in Rome

1556 - dies in Rome on 31 July.

Quotes

All to the greater glory of God

When in desolation, have patience and
consider that consolation will soon return.

When one enjoys consolation, let
him consider how he will conduct
himself during the time of desolation
which is to come.

There is no doubt that God will never
be wanting to us,
provided that He finds in us
that humility which makes us worthy
of his gifts,
the desire of possessing them, and
the eagerness to cooperate
willingly with the graces He gives us.

IGNATIUS LOYOLA

Ignatius was born in 1491 at Loyola in Spain, and was baptised "Inigo". The birth was extraordinarily providential. The year after Ignatius was born Christopher Columbus set sail on one of history's most daring expeditions to discover the new world. A whole new field of missionary endeavour opened up for the Church, and in God's providence a man had been born who would spearhead this mission. In 1517, when Ignatius was twenty six years old, Luther nailed his 95 theses against the Catholic faith to the Castle church at Wittenberg, beginning the Protestant Reformation. Ignatius was to experience his conversion in 1521, the same year that Luther was excommunicated at the Diet of Worms. Again it was the hand of God that the Companions of Jesus, which we now know as the Jesuits, formed by Ignatius, should play a major role in the Counter-Reformation, bringing theological competence to the Council of Trent and, more importantly, a practical, evangelical spirituality enabling the Catholic people to return to the initial fire of early Christianity.

Initial Conversion

As a young man, the son of a Lord, living in the Loyola castle, Ignatius was preoccupied with dreams of romance, chivalry, war, knighthood and love. At the age of thirty, and still unmarried, he enlisted in a local war with France. While defending a castle fortress at Pamplona a cannon ball passed between the young soldier's legs, shattering the right one and damaging the other. Captured by the enemy his wounds were treated for a while, but the French quickly handed the injured soldier back into the care of his fellow countrymen at Loyola castle. Doctors set to work on the legs by breaking them first and then re-setting them. Without anaesthetic, the treatment was excruciatingly painful. The young man almost died and received the sacramental anointing. Thankfully he survived the crude operation, but was dismayed that the procedure had left a bone protruding from the leg. For vanity's sake he ordered the surgeons to have the protrusion sawn off! This shows something of the darkness of his heart prior to conversion, but also something of his natural courage, even if it was for worldly gain.

During the time of his recuperation Ignatius was bored and had nothing to read. The household had no books of romance and chivalry which he would have enjoyed. There were only four volumes of the *Life of Christ* written by a Carthusian and a volume of the lives of the saints, composed by a Spanish author. As he read about the saints he began to experience what he later called "consolation".[81] Thinking about their rigorous lives under the "captaincy" of Jesus he found a joy and peace in his heart which lingered after his reading. In contrast he noted that when in his reveries he dwelt upon worldly pursuit of damsels, and achievements of grandeur in war, he experienced initial pleasure, but then found himself afterwards dry and discontented. Later he identified this as "desolation". He began to think, "What would happen if I should do things that St Francis and St Dominic did?" This thought led him to desire to make a complete break from his former worldly life and take up a rigorous life of penance. He was inspired to make a pilgrimage to Jerusalem to encounter Jesus in the very place where he walked the earth. One night he had a vision of Our Lady and the child Jesus which left him with a loathing for things of the flesh which had previously preoccupied his mind. The Holy Spirit was filling his heart with the fire of God's love. Now he wanted only to follow Jesus, to imitate him like the saints, and give his life for Jesus. The natural youthful energy for heroic deeds and romantic exploits was now, by the grace of God, being channelled towards becoming a radical disciple of Jesus.

Manresa Experience

Once he was able to walk again Ignatius set out for Montserrat, a monastery in the Pyrenees near Barcelona, where there was a famous image of the Black Madonna. On the way he gave away his fine clothes to a ragged tramp and put on sandals and a pilgrim tunic, which he had made for himself from some hemp linen. Arriving at the pilgrimage shrine he prayed through the night, preparing to make a general confession. It took him three days to write out all of his sins, and after confessing he felt wonderfully set free for the Lord. He then made his way to the small village of Manresa, where he lived in a cell in a Dominican monastery, but spent most of his time in caves, praying continuously and entering into intense spiritual battle. His only reading, apart from the gospels, was the *Imitation of Christ* by Thomas a Kempis, which became the basic spiritual book for his whole life. On the one hand his time in Manresa was a time of tranquillity and peace, as he spent seven hours in prayer each day, and sometimes through the night. On the other hand it was a time of interior battle when the evil one attempted to discourage him and lead him to despair. The enemy would taunt him, "How can you bear this for the rest of your life?"[82] He answered by reminding Satan that he would not promise him even one hour of his life. Having a finely tuned conscience Ignatius also suffered from scruples, doubting the validity of his previous confessions. Tortured with anxiety, at his lowest point he was even tempted to commit suicide. Although he tried many methods to overcome the scruples they persisted. Then finally without warning he received a grace from God and was suddenly delivered.

Ignatius recalls the revelations God gave him at Manresa. He was overcome with tears, when under the figure of three keys of an organ, he understood interiorly the beauty of the Trinity. On another occasion he delighted in the goodness of God in creating the world, and another when he saw rays of white light emanating from the elevated host, convincing him of the presence of Jesus in the Blessed Sacrament. Another time he "saw with inward eyes the humanity of Christ", and also the Blessed Virgin Mary. "He often thought to himself: Even if there were no Scripture which teaches these truths, he would be ready to die for them solely on the strength of what he had seen".[83] But the mystical experience which capped off all of his revelations occurred on the banks of the river Cardoner which flows close to Manresa. He recalls this foundational event in his autobiography. Writing about himself in the third person he remembers, "As he sat there the eyes of his understanding were opened and though he saw no vision he understood and perceived many things, numerous spiritual things as well as matters touching on faith and learning".[84]

This enlightenment was about things of faith, giving a fresh insight that was totally revolutionary for him. It was too much to write down, but this revelation shaped his whole life and became, no doubt, the basis of his *Spiritual Exercises* which he roughly composed at Manresa and then later edited and completed elsewhere. Three years before his death he recalls that in this moment of inspiration "he received such a lucidity in understanding that during the course of his entire life....if he were to gather all the helps he received from God and everything he knew, and add them together, he does not think they would add up to all that he received on that one occasion".[85] The *Spiritual Exercises* were the fruit of his desert experience at Manresa, including all the revelations, as well as the temptations and spiritual struggle he encountered there. While they were modified later, the substance of this amazing tool for conversion and discovering the will of God for one's life originated in this secluded time.

A Pilgrim Journey

Ignatius' initial vision for his life with God was simply to be a pilgrim to the Holy Land and to travel there, totally relying on the providence of God. After about a year and a half in Manresa he went first to Barcelona to prepare for the journey. He begged his passage and the necessary food. His journey took him by ship to Italy in order to gain permission from the Pope to go to the Holy Land, and then to Venice which was the port from which pilgrims usually embarked for Palestine. He reached the port of Jaffa in August 1523 and arrived in Jerusalem a month later. However, on arrival he was disappointed when the Franciscans refused to allow him to stay any longer than the normal time for a pilgrimage, just twenty days. Arriving back in Barcelona he was convinced from his journey of the need for study. He immediately set about learning Latin and in March 1526 he began to attend philosophy lectures at the University of Alcala.

Before leaving Barcelona an incident happened which speaks of the character that the Lord was forming in Ignatius. He loved to pray in the chapel of a convent of nuns, who had unfortunately relaxed their rule, allowing young men as visitors and taking the young sisters on pleasure trips and other scandalous activity. Ignatius felt called to reform the convent and began encouraging the sisters towards a more rigorous life in imitation of Jesus. The younger sisters in particular were persuaded by him and shut out the young men from visiting. The men were so infuriated they hired some Moors to beat up Ignatius and one of his companions. The attack was so furious that his companion died from his wounds and Ignatius himself was so near death that he was given the last rites.

At the University of Alcala Ignatius began to draw young men around him. His little group, dedicated to evangelical poverty, created suspicion, being cynically dubbed the "sack-wearers and illuminists".

They were reported to the Inquisition as "certain young men who go about in this town, clad in grey habits down to the ankles, some of them barefooted and who say that they live a life like that of the apostles". Ignatius was imprisoned, blamed for advising a woman and daughter to set off on a dangerous pilgrimage to the shrine of Our lady at Guadalupe near Portugal. Finally he was cleared of the false charge, but being released, he was warned to wear ordinary clothes and not to speak about matters of faith until he had finished four years of study. Moving to Salamanca in 1527 he came immediately under the scrutiny of the Dominicans. He was put under house arrest for three days in their priory, constantly interrogated, and then imprisoned. After 22 days of incarceration he and his three companions were released and given the approval to teach doctrine and speak about the things of God, but they were not permitted to explain the difference between mortal and venial sin until after four years of study. Ignatius found that too restrictive and decided to depart for the University of Paris, leaving his companions behind. He was now thirty seven years old and still intent on finishing his studies.

Conversions in Paris

At the University of Paris he was penniless, and was forced to support his studies by trips into Flanders to beg from the wealthy merchants and other well-heeled gentry. While studying in Paris he befriended young men, offering them the *Spiritual Exercises*, and guiding them through this classic tool of conversion therapy. The *Exercises* was a powerful means to form his men as disciples. Anyone who was a roommate to Ignatius became a target for his gentle persistent persuasion to undergo this unique spiritual program. Pierre Favre, Diego Lainez, Simon Rodriguez, and Alfonso Salmeron fell under his spell. Probably his biggest fish was Francis Xavier, a bright and rising academic star who came from Navarre. Francis was brilliant, charming and ambitious. Initially he scorned Ignatius' efforts to interest him in the new apostolate. After studying together for four years Francis was acclaimed as a scholar with a promising career ahead of him. Instead Ignatius was just a struggler academically. Noticing that Francis loved the limelight, Ignatius drew alongside him and joined in the applause, helping Francis to fulfil his ambitions. But wily Ignatius had a hidden motive for befriending this talented young man. Every now and then he would let slip before Francis the words of Jesus, "What does it profit a man if he gains the whole world and loses his very soul?" Francis' heart finally cracked open and he submitted to the *Exercises*, allowing Jesus to claim him and form him to be arguably the most ardent missionary the Church has ever seen.

Companions of Jesus

On 15 August, 1534 the six young men together with Ignatius gathered in the Chapel of the Martyrs in Montmartre to profess vows of poverty, chastity and obedience and to make a pilgrimage to the Holy Land. They were to assemble in Venice in three years' time and wait for a passage to the Holy Land. If after a year no passage was possible they were to present themselves to the Holy Father to be at his disposal. Before meeting in Venice they were destined to be joined by three others, Paschase Broet, Jean Codure and Claude Jay.

In 1537 when they met at Venice as planned and were awaiting a ship to the Holy Land they busied themselves preaching in the piazzas of various Italian cities. By this time they had all been ordained and they began to call themselves the Company of Jesus. This was not a military term but referred to companions or brothers. They agreed that their sole head was Jesus Christ, whom alone they wanted to serve. With no possibility of a ship leaving for Palestine due to the threat of Turkish intervention, Ignatius turned towards Rome with Favre and Lainez. As he travelled from Siena to Rome Ignatius felt in his heart that God was saying to him: "I will show you favour in Rome". He prayed to the Mother of God that her son would take him under his banner.

When they were only 15 kilometres out of Rome Ignatius went into the little church of La Storta on the Via Cassia to pray. There he experienced another vision like the one at the river Cordona. He saw Jesus with his cross on his shoulders and by his side the Father who said to Jesus, "I desire you to take this man for your servant". Jesus turned to Ignatius and said to him, "It is my will that you serve us". God the Father was uniting Ignatius closely with Jesus bearing the cross, and expressing his will that Ignatius should dedicate himself to their service. Ignatius was to be "placed with Christ" on the cross. In the middle of November 1537 they arrived in Rome, the Eternal City, which was to be home for Ignatius until his death at the age of sixty-five in 1556.

Detachment

At the beginning of the *Spiritual Exercises* Ignatius gives his "first principle and foundation" for everything that follows.[86] We will make progress in the spiritual life only if we learn detachment of heart from all created realities. We have been created out of love by God for a purpose: "to praise, reverence, and serve God our Lord, and by this means to save one's soul". All created things on this earth are meant to help us attain this purpose for which we are created. We are to make use of these things in so far as they help us to attain this end. We must rid ourselves of them in as far as they are obstacles to fulfilling this fundamental purpose.

It is important for our growth that we break with any inordinate attachments to created realities – whether they are things, persons, talents, relationships, dreams, or whatever. Genuine detachment of heart provides the space for us to be filled by God. Ignatius calls us to have a "holy indifference"; we are not to prefer health to sickness, riches to poverty, honour to dishonour, long life to short life. Whatever happens in our life it is most important that it works towards attaining our ultimate end. Our only desire and choice should be what is most conducive to the end for which we are created. When we are making a choice between two good possibilities, he says, we should always choose what is going to give greater glory to God.

Three Types of People

Ignatius helps us reflect on what degree of detachment we have by presenting three types of people.[87] The first type is those who have come to know the Lord and really desire to let go of their possessions, wanting to be free of unhealthy dependencies. But they keep putting off doing anything about it. They procrastinate, and at the hour of their death they still have not done what they intended to do. They were all good ideas, but no action. The second type of person is those who want to rid themselves of all attachments, but they want to do it on *their* terms, not on God's terms. They tend to hold on to those areas of their life which may be too difficult to give to God. They may even go so far as surrendering eighty or ninety percent to the Lord, but they hang on to the remainder and keep it under their control. They are full of good aspirations, but they still want to govern certain areas of their life themselves. They bargain with God, trying to buy him off. In areas of their life where the attachments are strongest they try to use God for their own ends, expecting him to dance to their tune, rather than surrendering fully to his will.

The third type of person actually embraces Christ fully in their lives, on his terms as he wills. They readily offer him all they have. They are willing to surrender their lives to the Lord on his terms. They bring all they have to the Lord and let him dispose of it as he wants. These people are keen to get rid of any attachment which hinders their union with God. Every decision is for the greater glory of God. Their desire is for whatever glorifies God, and they make their decisions accordingly. Ignatius' surrender prayer expresses this well.

> Take Lord receive,
> All my liberty, my memory, my understanding, my entire will,
> All I have and possess.
> You have given all to me. Now I return it. All is yours now.
> Dispose of it wholly according to your will.
> Give me only your love and your grace. That's enough for me.

This third attitude is the most desirable. The heart has a "holy indifference". Whatever the Lord wants is what matters. We give to him our lives and all they contain, letting him dispose of it all as he wills. We give him our health, our length of life, our manner of death, our gifts and talents, our family and friends, and all that is nearest and dearest to us. Then we seek to be indifferent about the way he disposes of these gifts in our life. Everything is to be for his glory. That's what matters. Jesus said: "…none of you can be my disciple unless he gives up all his possessions" (Luke 14:33). The Lord does not mean that he will lead us into a life of deprivation, but that we are to entrust to him the distribution of the goods. After all, everything is a gift from him anyway. Yet there is much in us that resists belonging to God in this way. We want to in some way control him. His love at work within us is constantly beckoning us to let go of the hold we have on everything, and to trust in the hold he has on us.

The call for a detached heart is not only about our attitude toward material possessions. It means all our relationships as well. Jesus says: "If any man comes to me without hating his father, mother, wife, children, brothers, sisters, yes his own life too, he cannot be my disciple" (Lk.14:26). Here the word "hate" is not referring to an emotion of enmity; but means an attitude of total detachment. It does not mean that we stop loving our family, but that this love must be subordinate to our love for Jesus and for his kingdom. To be wholly for Jesus we cannot be overly attached to anything, not even to our good works which we might do in order to advance the kingdom. Often we find out how attached we are to something when we are threatened with losing it. We find out how attached we have been to some project when it fails, and our whole world caves in with it! Ignatius was once asked how he would feel if the Pope disbanded the Jesuits which he had founded. He answered that he would need 15 minutes with the Lord, and then he would be fine. In other words he would need the time surrendering more deeply to the Lord in love; time to give back to the Lord what had been given to him.

Contemplation of the Gospels

St Ignatius' *Spiritual Exercises* provided a form of contemplative prayer adapted to the apostolic needs of the time. The word "contemplation" in the *Exercises* had a different meaning than its traditional use. For Ignatius contemplation consists in gazing upon a concrete object of the imagination; for example, recreating in the imagination a gospel scene and entering into the scene, hearing what people are saying, watching their actions, and responding appropriately within oneself. He encourages us to "look long" at Jesus with a loving attentive gaze. This is not a cold, analytical exercise. Rather the imagination is used to awaken an affective response in the heart, especially towards Jesus. Ignatius encourages us to apply the five senses to the subject of the meditation – seeking to hear, see, touch, taste, and smell what is happening in the scene. From this immersion into the scene, we are to gaze upon Jesus and be drawn into more intimate relationship with him, which will be transformative of our life. The more we meditate upon Jesus, and allow our hearts to be drawn into relationship with him, the more we will grow into his likeness.

It is good to appreciate the innovative quality of Ignatius' way of prayer. The Benedictines had already developed a way of praying with Scripture taken from the early desert Fathers called *lectio divina*, or divine reading. This method was designed to draw the heart into ever deeper levels of personal response to the word of God. In one period of prayer the person would read the text, meditate on it by chewing upon it, respond prayerfully, and allow the contemplative moment to occur, whereby the person rests in the knowledge of God's love. This way of prayer was never lost to the Church, but in places of learning in the medieval times the tendency was to concentrate on "mental prayer" with the focus on the work of the mind, without engaging the heart in encounter with God. By the high Middle Ages methods of interior prayer had become highly systematised into three different types of prayer: "discursive meditation", if thoughts predominated; "affective prayer", if the emphasis was on acts of the will; and "mystical contemplation", if graces were infused directly by God. This division was problematic, since contemplation was not seen as part of "mental prayer", but rather an extraordinary grace for mystics alone. Beginners were often taught discursive meditation alone, which was an intellectual exercise, providing many holy thoughts, but not serving to facilitate a personal encounter with the Lord.

The genius of the Ignatian way of prayer is that it brought the discursive, affective and contemplative dimensions of prayer back together again in one period of prayer. Thus, the person praying through an imaginative exercise was drawn by the Spirit into an affective response and a living "heart to heart" encounter with Jesus. The whole aim of the work of the imagination in constructing the scene of a gospel passage, and reflecting upon its significance, is to make affections of the will towards Jesus (e.g. love for him, zeal for souls, mercy, wonder, gratitude etc.). In this way of prayer the heart opens in loving relationship with Jesus. It is not just an exercise of *knowing about* Jesus, but of *knowing* him personally. It is an exercise of being with him so we can become more like him. The "looking long" at Jesus is the key to the more contemplative experience, a loving, attentive gaze upon him without having to rely any more on thoughts, imaginings or any vocal help.

Rules of Discernment

In his *Exercises* Ignatius offers rules for discerning the movements within the heart.

Ignatius considers that all interior movements of the heart come from either the "good spirit" or the "evil spirit". The "good spirit" is the action of the Holy Spirit. He refers to the "evil spirit" as all movements that are contrary to the work of God in the heart of the person. Ignatius would want everyone to grow in a discerning heart. This requires self-knowledge acquired over many years. We need to often scrutinize the heart to be in touch with its many conflicting movements. This is why Ignatius considered that the daily "examen" was more important even than contemplation for the growth of his companions. I will not go into detail here about the "examen" but it suffices to say that a daily exercise of reviewing the interior movements makes us sensitive to how God is moving within us at all times. We begin to experience his presence in all things. It also helps us be in touch with the confusion, negativity, and selfishness that can bring darkness to the heart, and the destructive thoughts and emotions which mislead us away from our journey to God.

The key to Ignatius' method of discernment is being able to detect "consolations" and "desolations". They are "felt states" of the soul. Earlier I described how Ignatius first became aware of these movements within him when he was reading the life of Christ and the lives of the saints while recuperating in Loyola Castle. They cannot be identified with any particular thought or emotion, but thoughts ,emotions , desires and attitudes flow from these states of being. Ignatius says:

> I call it consolation when an interior movement is aroused in the soul, by which it is inflamed with love of its Creator and Lord, and as a consequence, can love no creature on the face of the earth for its own sake, but only in the Creator of them all. It is likewise consolation when one sheds tears that move to the love of God, whether it be because of sorrow for sins, or because of the sufferings of Christ our Lord, or for any other reason that is immediately directed to the praise and service of God. Finally, I call consolation every increase of faith, hope and love, and all interior joy that invites and attracts to what is heavenly and to the salvation of one's soul by filling it with peace and quiet in its Creator and Lord.[88]

The most common experience of consolation is the felt state of peace in the Lord, and interior joy drawing us to Jesus, and a sense of increase in faith, hope and love. Desolation is a felt state of the heart which is the exact opposite. Ignatius says it is:

> ...darkness of soul, turmoil of spirit, inclination to what is low and earthly, restlessness rising from many disturbances and temptations which lead to want of faith, want of hope,

want of love. The soul is wholly slothful, tepid, sad, and separated, as it were, from its Creator and Lord. For just as consolation is the opposite of desolation, so the thoughts that spring from consolation are the opposite of those that spring from desolation.[89]

Desolation can be a very confused and stormy experience, or just a sense of feeling "blah". What characterises it most of all is a lack of peace, a heaviness of spirit, and a distaste for the things of God. Ignatius says that desolation never comes from God, even though the Lord allows it to happen. On the other hand, consolation can be true or false, depending on whether it comes from God or is conjured up by the evil spirit. Ignatius' first set of rules are intended for people who are in the early stages of breaking with sin, the devil, the world and the flesh, and are earnest in giving themselves to the Lord. Here the primary challenge is to learn to deal with desolation. The tactic of the evil spirit in these early stages of the journey is to bring discouragement. Ignatius says that for those who are striving to break with their former life and embrace the new life in Jesus "it is characteristic of the evil spirit to harass with anxiety, to afflict with sadness, to raise obstacles backed by fallacious reasoning that disturbs the soul. Thus he seeks to prevent the soul from advancing". This first set of rules seeks to give common sense guidelines which help us to avoid giving up and throwing in the towel when desolation occurs.

Working on Desolation

The first important rule is that we never change a resolution or make a major decision when we are experiencing desolation.[90] Since desolation always comes from the evil spirit, Ignatius says that this would be tantamount to making the devil your spiritual director! Commentators agree that if beginners could remember this rule they would be saved from much of the confusion that can come into their lives. Another important rule is to move in the opposite spirit to the desolation. Because we feel rotten we are likely to be governed by this and give up praying, or at least cut it back. Ignatius counsels to increase our spiritual activity, and to do more prayer and penance rather than to slacken off. He says that while we may not clearly perceive it, the Lord always gives us the grace sufficient to resist the desolation. So we should persevere in patience, and be confident that consolation will return in time.

Ignatius offers three reasons why the Lord allows desolation to take place. While the Lord is not the author of the desolation, in his provident care of us he permits it to happen, so that, with our cooperation, he can draw good fruit from it. The first reason is because we have become negligent, lethargic and indifferent in our spiritual life. The desolation comes as a salutary shock. It can be used to shake us out of our torpor and bring us to repentance and back to a whole-hearted commitment. In time of desolation we need to check our hearts to see if this is the reason for our plight. If so, it is a matter of humbly repenting, and the desolation will lift. If, upon checking our hearts, this is not the case, there are two other possible reasons for the desolation. The Lord may want to test us by the purifying our faith and love for him. We are not to live by feelings but by faith. When the Lord allows the feelings to become distasteful and disturbing, he strengthens our faith which is not dependent on feelings. Similarly, with the withdrawal of consolations and favours, we learn to love by a decision of the will, rather than by affections.

The final reason why the Lord allows desolation is to humble us. He wants to teach us that consolation is pure gift from him. Early in the journey he spoils us with consolations, because he is winning us to himself. After a while, we tend to subtly think that we are doing it by ourselves. So the Lord "pulls the rug from under our feet", and we now feel our utter poverty, and how incapable we are of doing anything for our salvation. We experience more acutely that all is gift from the Lord. We find ourselves necessarily having to cry out to him in earnest for help. We grow in humility.

Discerning Consolation

The second set of rules deals with discerning between true and false consolations. There is only one type of consolation that is definitely from God and beyond question. This is what Ignatius calls "consolation without previous cause".[91] He means by this that the consolation comes totally "out of the blue", without any previous perception or knowledge. Most consolations do have a preceding cause. For example, we can trace the insight we had in prayer to a book we were reading the previous day, or we can be brought into a consoling moment of the Lord's embrace through meditation on a scripture text, or we can be filled with love for the Creator as we watch a beautiful sunset. Anything that has been prompted by our own acts of intellect or imagination or senses has a "preceding cause". This is God's normal way of communicating with us. So it is rare to have consolation *without* previous cause. Consequently, we need to pray for discernment of our consolations, since some of them do not have the stamp of God upon them. We need to check their credentials.

The evil spirit can assume the guise of the "angel of light". Ignatius says:

> He begins by suggesting thoughts that are suited to a devout soul, and ends by suggesting his own. For example, he will suggest holy and pious thoughts that are wholly in conformity with the sanctity of the soul. Afterwards, he will endeavour little by

little to end by drawing the soul into his hidden snares and evil designs.[92]

As the "angel of light" the evil spirit can produce ecstasies and visions, can foster for his own ends noble and great works, and can stoke for his own designs great apostolic zeal. However, he can only mimic the consolations of God. He can never replicate them in their purity. For the discerning heart the "tail of the serpent" is always evident. The evil spirit's "finger prints" will mar his cleverest forgeries. We need to be able to detect these forgeries, to be good "money-changers". The Holy Spirit will always be inspiring us towards greater love of God, obedience to his will and humility. The evil spirit will have a different end. Ultimately, we can only tell the soundness of the tree from its fruits. We may have been thoroughly convinced that a particular course of action was inspired by God, but if it ends up in self-centred, ambitious posturing before others, we would have to question whether it was truly inspired by God at all. A friendship that blossoms may seem to be given by God, since it has opened up a deeper sense of affection for God, but if it takes us away from our commitment in marriage or in the celibate state, we would have to conclude that it was simply manipulated by the evil spirit for his own ends. An initial intense fervour for God and profound zeal for holiness can gradually over time be diverted into a false self-righteousness and "holier than thou" attitude, and an almost angry denunciation of others who are not so 'enlightened'. This sort of bad fruit is a clear indication of the evil spirit's presence, even though the person may still profess to be very zealous for the Lord and for his Kingdom.

Making Decisions in the Lord

Life is full of decisions. This teaching is about making a significant choice between two good options for one's life. Ignatius offers us three modes of making the decision.[93] The first is when clarity is given immediately by God and we have no doubt about what we must do. In Ignatius' words, "God so moves and attracts the will that, without doubting or being able to doubt, the devout soul follows what is shown to it, as St Paul and St Matthew did in following Christ our Lord".[94] There is a certitude and deep peace which comes with this revelation. As an example we can think of the word which Mother Teresa received "out of the blue" while on the train to Darjeeling which convinced her of her new vocation, or the word of the gospel which St Francis heard in St Mary of the Angels church. At once he cried out, "This is what I want, this is what I seek, this is what I want to do with all my heart!" He did not need any further consultation. He knew what he must do.

The second mode of decision-making is through attention to the movements of the heart.[95] How is the Spirit leading? How is Jesus drawing my heart? It involves discerning what is happening during the movements of consolation and desolation. If during consolation we find the heart drawn to a particular path then it is a good indication of the drawing of the Lord. However, we need to be sure that it is genuine consolation and not a false sweetness provided by the evil spirit. On the other hand, if we find an attraction to a particular direction while in desolation we cannot be sure whether it is true or not. During desolation the evil spirit is more likely to dissuade us from the way God is leading us. We ought not make any decisions at all when in desolation since we may well be using the evil spirit as our spiritual director! If over a period of time there is a consistent drawing to a particular option when we are experiencing consolation then we may readily choose that path.

Ignatius is aware that the second way of discerning a decision is not always conclusive. We are sometimes left in doubt and unsure of what is the right way to go. Consequently, he offers a third mode.

Interestingly, he spends more time describing this mode, probably because he realised that many people would need to resort to it. There are some conditions that he lays before us first. It needs to be a time of tranquillity, "that is, a time when the soul is not agitated by different spirits, and has free and peaceful use of its natural powers". Another condition is that we refresh ourselves in the foundational principle which I described earlier, so that we truly desire that the decision made is according to God's will and is to his greater glory. We want the decision to be truly in the service of the Lord and the salvation of souls. Ignatius says to weigh up the advantages and disadvantages of each option as objectively as possible, seeking to maintain indifference to the outcome. This is meant to be a prayerful exercise. After a time of reflection on the pros and cons of each option a decision can be made for which alternative seems reasonable. Then it is a matter of seeking the Lord in prayer to ask him for confirmation of the decision.

Forever practical, Ignatius suggests that if this process gets stuck, then imagine yourself advising someone else whom you want to see grow in holiness. What would you advise that person? He also suggests to prayerfully imagine yourself at the moment of death, or on the Day of Judgment. Which decision would you like to have made? The key to making any decision is a genuinely surrendered heart to the will of God.

To the Ends of the Earth

While Ignatius never left Rome after arriving there in 1537 the fire which the Lord had lit in his heart went to the ends of the earth. If you visit the church of Sant'Ignazio in Rome, tucked away in a myriad of alleyways and piazzas, you can put a coin into a machine on the wall and the wonderful fresco covering the whole the ceiling of the nave will be illuminated. In breathtaking colour, populated with people of all continents, the fresco, painted in 1685 by Andrea Pozzo, a Jesuit brother, depicts the missionary work of Ignatius and his early companions. In the centre of the picture we see the Risen Christ and from his pierced side emanate rays of light which enter the heart of Ignatius, setting him on fire. Then from Ignatius the light radiates to the four corners of the fresco, representing the four continents then known. The peoples of each continent are dressed in the costumes of their culture and are easily identified as Europeans, Asians, Africans and Americans. Around the edges of the fresco in large gold letters are the words of Jesus, "I have come to bring fire to the earth, and how I wish it were blazing already" (Lk 12:49). This is a magnificent artistic depiction of the mystery of God's immense love so overwhelming the heart of Ignatius that it must go forth to the whole world. Ignatius himself did not carry the good news to other continents, but the Lord captured the hearts of his followers through their immersion into the fire of God's love in the *Exercises* and then sent them out to all the nations.

The history of Spirit-filled evangelisation by the Jesuits is well known. If the fire of God's love made manifest in Jesus crucified captures the hearts of young men they become unstoppable with self-sacrificing love and willingness even to die for the sake of the salvation of others. Examples abound, but maybe to mention just a few. When Ignatius suddenly announced to his secretary, Francis Xavier, that he must head to Portugal to catch a ship that was leaving for India, Francis did not hesitate a moment. When they parted, never to see one another again, Ignatius is reputed to have said to his friend, "Go, set all afire!" After a harrowing year- long journey around the Cape, during which many on the ship died from disease, Francis arrive in Goa in the Spring of 1542. From there he made his way to Cape Comorin, 600 miles away. From this remote location he wrote to Ignatius his famous letter:

> How many in these countries fail to become Christians simply for the lack of a teacher of the Christian faith! Often I think of running through the universities of Europe and principally Paris and the Sorbonne, there to shout at the top of my voice like one who had lost his senses – to tell those men whose learning is greater than their wish to put their knowledge to good use, how many souls, through their negligence, must lose heaven and end up in hell. If all who, with so much labour, study letters, would pause to consider the account they must one day render to God concerning the talents entrusted to them, I am sure that they would come to say: 'Here I am Lord. Send me where you please, even to India'.[96]

Amazingly Francis' missionary life was only ten short years before he died off the coast of China, full of desire to bring the good news to that land as well. In such a brief time he had missioned around the coast of Southern India, then to the Spice Islands in Malaysia, and from there to Japan. In Japan, needing to gain permission to preach, he made a long, arduous journey through the snow to meet with the Emperor, only to find out that the power to allow the spreading of the faith really lay with the local daimyos. Undaunted, he threw away his tattered clothing, donned Japanese clothes and approached the local rulers bearing expensive gifts. Gradually conversions happened. But having heard about the huge field of unbaptised people in China Francis pressed on to this ultimate goal. He died on 21 November 1552 on a windy deserted island in the mouth of the Canton River.

Paul Miki

One fruit of Francis' mission to Japan was Paul Miki, born in 1564. When he was four years old his parents converted to Christianity. By this time there were hundreds of thousands of Christians in Japan.

But Christianity was seen to be a religion of foreigners and was held in suspicion. Often the Japanese rulers would clamp down on the new faith, persecuting its followers. Paul Miki, as a young man, decided to become a Jesuit. In 1587 a Japanese general, Hideyoshi, seized power, and he issued an edict banning Jesuit missionaries. However the order was not fully implemented, so evangelising work still continued underground. But then in the fall of 1596 a Spanish ship from Manila foundered on the coast of Japan. A loose comment by the captain enraged Hideyoshi. Police barged into the Jesuit residence at Osaka and arrested Paul and his companions. They were sentenced to death by crucifixion. Twenty four of these young men were put on a forced march from Osaka to Nagasaki, where the bulk of Christians lived. On the way they were grossly insulted and beaten as they passed through one village after another. On the day of execution in a wheat field outside of Nagasaki the Christians of the town assembled. The martyrs were each tied to a cross with metal bands and ropes. Then crosses were lifted and slid into the holes made in the ground for them. Throughout their ordeal the martyrs were singing "Praise the Lord, you children of the Lord". The whole crowd began chanting, "Jesus, Mary. Jesus, Mary". The executioners moved from one victim to the other, giving a guttural shout and then slaughtering each by a sword thrust through the heart. Before this bloody ritual began Paul Miki pronounced his final testimony in the form of a samurai farewell song:

> I did not come from the Philippines. I am Japanese by birth, and a brother of the Society of Jesus. I have committed no crime. The only reason I am condemned to die is that I taught the gospel of our Lord Jesus Christ. I am happy to die for such a cause and accept death as a great gift from my Lord. At this critical time, when you can rest assured that I will not try to deceive you, I want to stress and make it unmistakably clear that man can find no way to salvation other than the Christian way.[97]

He then went on to forgive his enemies and declared his desire that all his persecutors be converted to the Christian faith. When John Paul II visited Nagasaki he renamed this location "Resurrection Hill", declaring that the victory of Paul Miki and his companions was a share in the victory of Jesus on the Cross which has won for us love over hatred and goodness over evil.

North American Martyrs

There has been an endless stream of blood shed by the Jesuit martyrs for the sake of Jesus and his kingdom. Since we have accredited Ignatius with spearheading the proclamation of the gospel to the "new world", it would be appropriate to move from Asia to North America as one further witness of the extraordinary fruit of his surrender to the Lord. There is a small town in northern New York State called Auriesville where in the eighteenth century the fierce Mohawk Indians had a large village named Ossernenon. Today the visitor can walk through a serene forest of large oak trees where the village used to be. Each of the trees has the name of Jesus carved into the bark in large red lettering. This was the place where Isaac Jogues, a Jesuit missionary and his companion Rene Goupil had been kept captive and treated with contempt as the squaws for years.[98] They had made a pact with one another that whenever they were to be put to death, which could happen at any time, they would die with the name of Jesus on their lips. The fateful moment came for Rene, a lay brother, when a young brave for no real reason hacked his head open with a tomahawk. Isaac in his diary records the courageous death with great joy because Rene had been true to his promise and uttered the name of Jesus as he gasped his last breath.

The significance of the name of Jesus on the trees today remembers their sacred pact, but also recalls that Isaac, during his captivity, whenever possible would carve the name of Jesus on the trees around the camp, trusting that by his holy name the powers of Satan which held this people enslaved would be ultimately broken. Isaac was to endure captivity for eight years before he managed to escape and find a boat to his homeland in France. Back in Europe he was a celebrity amongst kings and queens because he carried on his body the visible scars of the brutal torture he had undergone at the merciless hands of the Indians. But he cared little for the honour given him and begged his superiors to allow him to return to the mission, since a fire burned within him to bring the good news of God's love to these ferocious tribes. Finally, he had the opportunity to return, and almost immediately he was captured again, by the Mohawks, together with his companion Jean de Lalande.

They set upon the two men, stripped them naked, and beat them furiously. They cut strips from Isaac's neck and arms. Isaac kept protesting that he came in peace and simply wanted to show them the way to heaven. That night as Isaac was sitting in the tent waiting to know his fate, an Indian brave approached and invited him to a feast. To refuse would be a great offence, but a friendly squaw warned him that this could be a trap. All the same he went to the lodge, and as he bent his head down to enter the tent another brave struck him with a hatchet. He fell at the feet of his murderer with the name of Jesus on his lips. They then finished the work by hacking off his head and dragging his body through the camp with glee. Jean Lalande was killed in a similar way the next morning and their bodies were thrown into the river, while their heads were displayed on the palisade which enclosed the village.

A wonderful sequel to this gruesome story is that in the next generation many of these people were to profess faith in Christ, and from this very village has come the "flower of the Mohawks", Kateri Tekakwitha, who was the first Native American to be recognized as a saint. Kateri was born in 1656 in Ossernenon, only ten years after Isaac's death. Her mother was a Christian of another tribe, who had been captured and chosen as a wife for the Mohawk chief. Unfortunately, all of Kateri's family died when she was still young during a smallpox outbreak. Kateri survived but with deep scars on her body as a result of the disease. She was brought up by her uncle, but at the age of nineteen she converted to Christianity with the help of Jesuit missionaries. Her decision was so unpopular that it put her life in danger. She had to escape to a Christian village, only living for another five years. Her story reminds us of Tertullian's saying, "the blood of martyrs is the seed of Christians".

TERESA OF AVILA

Chronology
1515 - born in Avila, Spain
1535 - joined convent of Incarnation in Avila
1562 - established reformed convent of St Joseph
1567 - wrote *"The Life"* and *"The Way of Perfection"*
1577 - wrote "Interior Castle"
1582 - died on 4 October at Alba de Tormes, Spain

Quotes

Let nothing disturb you;

nothing frighten you.

All things are passing.

God never changes.

Patience obtains all things.

Nothing is wanting to him

who possesses God.

God alone suffices.

Mental prayer in my opinion is

nothing else than an intimate sharing

 between friends; it means taking time

 frequently to be alone with Him

who we know loves us.

The important thing is not to
think much, but to love much.

Perfection consists not in consolations
but in the increase of love.

TERESA OF AVILA

Teresa was born in Avila on 28 March, 1515, twenty four years after Ignatius of Loyola, and in the heady early days of the Protestant Reformation. With the Church in crisis, the Holy Spirit birthed two major movements, one through Ignatius that was destined to take the gospel to the "new world" and the other through Teresa that was to charter more deeply the inner journey of the soul. Interestingly, both began their life work in their later years. Ignatius was forty eight when his companions were established as a religious order. Teresa was fifty two when she opened the new St Joseph's convent in Avila under the original Carmelite rule. This met with strong opposition but eventually she prevailed. With enormous courage and vigour she founded sixteen new convents throughout Spain according to the Rule of the discalced Carmelites, setting in motion, together with John of the Cross, a new awakening of contemplative prayer, and leaving at her death in 1582 at the age of sixty seven a legacy of spiritual writings which remain an essential source for anyone serious about the journey of prayer.

Entry into the Convent

Teresa seems to have had a normal childhood and teenage years with dreams of romance and chivalry, cultivating her feminine charms to win a noble suitor. At the age of sixteen she was entrusted to the care of the Augustinian sisters of Our Lady of Grace in Avila. Here she learnt cooking, sewing, embroidery and other such feminine arts considered necessary for marriage. However, one of the nuns became an inspiring spiritual influence over Teresa, and the impressionable young woman's thoughts turned towards becoming a nun. This growing aspiration was encouraged by an uncle who lived as a hermit. So on 2 November, 1535, at the age of twenty she secretly left her father's house to join the convent of the Incarnation in Avila. Her father soon came around to the idea and supported her with a generous dowry which enabled her to possess her own room in the convent. There were about one hundred and eighty women in the convent, many from noble families. They were able to have servants and could freely entertain visitors. It was not a convent of strict observance, but then it would not be entirely accurate to say the nuns lived a totally worldly way of life. They had a routine of celebrating the Divine Office with solemnity, maintained times for silent prayer, and had certain days of fasting. Yet it seems from Teresa's testimony they received no instruction on interior prayer. Consequently the spirituality was superficial, formalistic and lacking in substance.

Teresa enjoyed the way of life of the convent, but after three years she became seriously ill and almost died. She attributed her miraculous healing to St Joseph whom she had invoked to help her in her lowest moment. While she was recuperating she was given a copy of Francisco de Osuna's *Third Spiritual Alphabet*, which was one of the few spiritual books at that time which taught about being recollected in prayer. She devoured the book and passed it on to others. Inspired by the author she began to work on meditation. However, she found it to be an excruciating battle. The practice of prayer was almost impossible. Writing later about these years of dogged persistence in prayer she recalls: "And very often, for some years, I was more anxious that the hour I had determined to spend in prayer be over than I was to remain there....and so unbearable was the sadness I felt on entering the oratory, that I had to muster up all my courage".[99] During the time for prayer she would work hard at discursive meditation, attempting to concentrate on the topic of the meditation, thinking of holy things, and hoping to gain from the experience. But it only brought distractions and frustration.

Then after twenty years of seemingly endless struggle in prayer a breakthrough occurred unexpectedly. At the age of forty she experienced the onset of the "prayer of recollection". This is her account of how it happened:

> One day entering the oratory I saw a statue they had borrowed for a certain feast to be celebrated in the house. It represented the much wounded Christ and was very devotional so that beholding it I was utterly distressed in seeing him that way, for it well represented what he suffered for us. I felt so keenly aware of how poorly I thanked him for those wounds that, it seems to me, my heart broke. Beseeching him to strengthen me once and for all that I might not offend him, I threw myself down before him with the greatest outpouring of tears… I think I then said that I would not rise from there until He granted what I was begging him for. I believe certainly this was beneficial to me, because from that time I went on improving.[100]

Since she could not reflect discursively with the intellect, she learnt to image Christ within her, especially in scenes from the passion when he was suffering alone. Her favourite scene was Jesus in the Garden of Gethsemane. From that time onwards she always carried around with her a picture of the suffering Christ to help stimulate her recollection.

Around the same time as she discovered the prayer of recollection she read the *Confessions* of St Augustine. She says:

> It seems to me I saw myself in them…..When I came to the passage where he speaks about his conversion and read how he heard that voice in the garden, it only seemed to me, according to what I felt in my heart, that it was I the Lord called. I remained for a long time totally dissolved in tears and feeling within myself utter distress and weariness. Oh, how a soul suffers, God help me, by losing the freedom it should have in being itself; and what torments it undergoes! I marvel now at how I could have lived in such great affliction. May God be praised who gave me life to rise up from a death so deadly".[101]

In both these instances Teresa was experiencing the grace of compunction which leads us to weep for our sinfulness, not in a bitter attitude of self-reproach, but rather with the warmth of knowing the utter mercy of God which we do not deserve. It was a time in her journey when a major interior shift was happening. Prayer was no longer an intellectual exercise, but an encounter with Jesus and an opening of the heart in love for her Saviour. This description of the experience of recollection, which ultimately leads to infused contemplation, is one of Teresa's greatest spiritual legacies which we need to draw upon.

Woman of Courage

Before offering a few insights from Teresa's teaching on prayer it will be worthwhile to get in touch with the sort of woman she was. In 1561, Teresa, now aged forty six years, was inspired to found a new convent of strict observance in Avila. While she gained initial approval from the Carmelite Order, her fellow nuns, the local nobility, the magistrates and others united in vigorous opposition determined to thwart the project. Teresa was undaunted. One of Teresa's married sisters began with her husband to erect a building for the new convent, ostensibly as a house intended for the family. During the construction her little nephew was crushed by a wall which fell on him as he was playing. When they carried the lifeless body to Teresa, she took him in her arms and prayed. He was immediately restored. After a tortuous struggle with local authorities she finally gained permission to have the Blessed Sacrament in the little chapel, and four novices took the habit.

After five peaceful years with thirteen nuns in her little convent of St Joseph, Teresa founded another convent in Media del Campo, and then in Valladolid, and Toledo. There was no stopping the determination of this intrepid woman. When beginning the work at

Toledo she had only five ducats, the equivalent of ten dollars. She was heard to say, "Teresa and this money are nothing; but God, Teresa and these ducats suffice". Over a period of fifteen years Teresa travelled extensively around Spain establishing fourteen new convents, three of them in her last year before death. She was indomitable. This was an astonishing achievement for a small, enfeebled woman. Travelling in a curtained carriage or cart over pot-holed roads, her trips took her from the Northern provinces down to the Mediterranean, and west into Portugal, across mountains, rivers and arid plateaus. Enduring all these hardships in a harsh climate and rough and ready lodgings at night, and little food to sustain her, she also had to deal with considerable opposition to many of her foundations.

From all of this we gain a picture of a courageous woman of strong character, a good sense of humour, ever practical, shrewd in dealing with corrupt businessmen, sharp in her perception of others, relying totally on the providence of God, and fully committed to the work of the reform. An amusing incident often told about Teresa was when she and her companions were travelling with a cart loaded with gear to establish a new house. As they were crossing a ford the rush of water was stronger than they expected and the cart with all the gear was swept down the river. Always in conversation with the Lord, Teresa complained to him, "If you allow this to happen to your friends, no wonder you have so few!" It's good for us to be in touch with this feisty woman who was a great mystic. Teresa's earthiness makes us realise that the interior life is not some esoteric, other-worldly journey, but a movement into the heart which bears fruit in genuine practical love.

Entering into Prayer

Teresa says, "Though we are always in the presence of God it seems to me the manner is different with those who practice prayer, for they are aware that He is looking at them. With others, it can happen that several days pass without their recalling that God sees them".[102] This reminds us that quiet prayer of the heart is simply looking at Jesus with attentive love, but even more so it is being aware that he is looking at me with infinite love. That makes all the difference because we come to know ourselves as known and loved by God.

If we are enamoured by the world with all its attractions we will find it hard for our hearts to enter into prayer. We need to be before prayer what we want to be at prayer. A detachment from worldly things will allow the soul the space to draw aside and encounter God. It does not mean physically withdrawing from our responsibilities in the world, but it calls for an attitude of heart which is not bound unduly to worldly concerns. We must be free so the Lord can be enthroned at the deepest level of our being. She defines prayer as "nothing else than an intimate sharing between friends; it means taking time frequently to be alone with Him who we know loves us".[103] It would be a peculiar friendship if there was no intimate sharing. We need to come in our weakness with all our struggles and pour our heart out to the Lord, and allow him to meet us with tenderness and mercy. Teresa is clear that it is not enough to pray in the midst of our many activities. While seeking to practice the presence of God at all times is good, this will not be sustained and deepened without regular times aside in solitude with the Lord alone. As we become more accustomed to dwelling in Christ within the soul we will find that often during the day we will become aware of his presence and yield to him in love.

Teresa insists that to begin the interior journey well one needs to be utterly determined never to give up, no matter what trials or temptations come our way. She coaches her sisters to endure in the spiritual journey no matter what:

I say that how they are to begin is very important – in fact, all important. They must have a great and very resolute determination to persevere until reaching the end, come what may, happen what may, whatever work is involved, whatever criticism arises, whether they arrive or whether they die on the road, or even if they don't have courage for the trials that are met, or even if the whole world collapses.[104]

We need to be single-minded in purpose, courageous in the face of opposition, with a very determined determination never to give way to the suggestions of the evil one or to the temptations from others, and not to allow calamities to deter us from the path we have chosen.

Finding Who I am in God

Prayer she says consists of being aware of who we are before God, and being aware of who God is for us, and daring to speak with him.[105] All three dynamics are important. By being aware of who we are she means our nothingness before God who created us and sustains us in being. It means also our existential condition right now, not some theoretical concept of our existence. It refers to how I am now, what my present experience is like. The only way to come to prayer is in humility, which Teresa understands to be truth. We must come with authenticity, real honesty before the Lord, not hiding anything or trying to look good before him. Rather than being like the proud Pharisee at the front of the temple we must come as the penitent tax collector, meeting the Lord in the truth of our weakness, fragility and brokenness, but confident in his mercy. Being aware of who God is means that we know him to be totally trustworthy and full of mercy. He comes to comfort the broken hearted and to bring healing to the wounded. We dare to speak to him because even though he is Majestic God on high, who holds the whole universe in his hands, he has been revealed to us by Jesus as our loving Father. We can confidently throw ourselves into his loving arms.

Teresa was in touch with her own struggle to be virtuous; and felt deeply her inability to be good, true and holy. She struggled with her sinfulness, having a great desire for union with God, but a blatant inability to live up to those desires. This interior struggle within herself led her more deeply to encounter Christ. Filled with anxieties, overwhelmed by difficulties and problems, she found in prayer that her mind and emotions would take over. What could she do? It seemed impossible to pray. In her broken human condition she turned to Jesus. How she loved to be with Jesus in the Garden of Gethsemane! Why? Because she experienced him suffering with her, sharing in her own human struggle. This is why the Son of God became human. He took to himself our humanity so he knows now what it is like to struggle as we do. He shares our experience of what it is to be human. When she experienced her inability to pray because of her interior battles with her brokenness, Teresa learnt to turn to him who was waiting for her in his humanity, suffering with her, and bringing light to her darkness. Her very inability to pray led her to meet Jesus and sit with him, and look at him being with her with such great love.

When we, in our broken humanity, are struggling with things that seem to be beyond our control, we need to come to Jesus. In our very brokenness he draws us into ourselves, not to focus on our problems, but so that we can meet him. He shares our humanity and gives us hope in the midst of our struggle. Rather than fall into depression about our weaknesses we can allow the Spirit to draw us into the inner chamber of our heart where we can meet Jesus who is with us in our struggle and brings us hope. So prayer is a meeting of friends; Jesus wants us to come to him just as we are, no frills attached, and look into his eyes of mercy as we open to him the pain of our broken human existence. His compassion is total because he shares with us the burden of our humanity. Through this living encounter with him we come to know ourselves as known and loved by God. In bringing our own experience of our broken humanity to Jesus, we begin to know and love ourselves as God loves us.

No matter how far we go in the journey of prayer it is critically important for Teresa that we do not lose touch with the humanity of Jesus. By encountering the humanity of Jesus, especially in his passion, we learn how to be ourselves. True spirituality does not make us more angelic; rather it keeps us earthed in our existential human reality. In our broken human condition we come to Jesus in his humanity and open our hearts to him, finding in him the consolation that we seek and our true identity as known and loved by God. Our friendship with Jesus is not some spiritualised disincarnate reality. "What more do we desire than to have such a good friend at our side, who will not abandon us in our labours and tribulations…Blessed are they who truly love him and always keep him at their side?"[106]

Recollection

For Teresa, wherever God is, there is heaven. So if God is dwelling in the soul, then to that extent we are already experiencing heaven. The prayer of recollection is simply going into the depths of our soul and looking at the Guest within that place, and not turning away from him. He awaits us in that inner place. With great humility we can meet him and speak to him with love. She calls this sort of prayer recollection "because the soul collects its faculties together and enters within itself to be with God. And its divine Master comes to teach it and give it the prayer of quiet more quickly than he would through any other method it might use".[107] Here Teresa is describing this prayer of recollection as the beginning of contemplation which flowers ultimately as the prayer of quiet, when the will becomes captive to the love of God. She encourages all who want to go deeper in prayer to "enclose themselves within this little heaven of our soul, where the Master of heaven and earth is present, and grow accustomed to refusing to be where the exterior senses in their distraction have gone…".[108]

Teresa does not want us to "strain the brain with long drawn out reflections". She says, "I am not asking you to do anything more than look at him…". In order to move into recollection she encourages the use of a picture, or to imagine a scene in the passion of Jesus, or read something from a book, as a way of prompting the movement inward. Teresa does not mean that we are to be in control of the movement as if we have a technique that always works for us. It is really the work of God. She likens it to a shepherd whose whistle draws back the wandering sheep.[109] It is as if the soul hears the gentle call of the Shepherd's whistle, who is already within the soul, and heeds it as an almost irresistible drawing on the heart. The person praying becomes less and less dependent on the use of any exterior help as the soul longs more and more to dwell within the presence of the Lord. Recollection is not acquired by the intellect thinking of the things of God, nor by the imagination seeking to excite the soul. These techniques are now rendered somewhat useless. She says "the important thing is not to think much but to love much; and so do that which best stirs you to love".[110]

Prayer of Quiet

The prayer of recollection disposes us for the gift of infused contemplation (the prayer of quiet). While the prayer of recollection is a method of turning the eyes inward within oneself and discovering the Master within, and seeking to dwell in the heaven that is already in our hearts, the prayer of quiet cannot be induced in any way. It is a purely supernatural infilling of God's love. "This prayer is something supernatural, something we cannot procure through our own efforts. In it the soul enters into peace or, better, the Lord puts it at peace by his presence".[111] In this moment of quiet "a person feels the greatest delight in his body and a great satisfaction in his soul". This "delight" is not in any way a sensual feeling, but belongs to the "intimate part of the soul" and is sheer gift from God. It cannot be engendered by our own interior efforts, nor by external stimuli such as music, liturgical beauty, preaching or whatever. By God's grace alone the will becomes captive to love and the person simply wants to stay still, dwelling with love in the presence of the Beloved. It seems that all their desires are fulfilled; the heart is expanded in love. The person wants to be nowhere else than in this state of quiet peace and tranquillity. The love of God enflames the soul which is devoid of self-interest and has a new detachment from worldly pleasures.

The journey from the prayer of recollection to the prayer of quiet is not a quantum leap from one state to another. Rather, Teresa seems to talk about it as a gradual transition. The efforts to recollect become more passive and receptive without having to work at making it happen. She describes recollection from the beginning as something that the Lord brings about as he draws us into himself, but which we actively foster in response to this grace. The soul collects its faculties together and enters within itself to be with its God. Already passive contemplation is occurring. During this time when passive prayer of recollection is beginning we can gently keep the fire burning by an occasional vocal prayer, repetition of a biblical word, or holding an image from the passion of Jesus, as a way of maintaining receptivity to the infusion of grace. She says, "at most a gentle word from time to time is sufficient, as in the case of one who blows on a candle to enkindle it again when it begins to die out".[112] As the prayer of quiet develops it is important not to blow too hard otherwise the candle will be extinguished. Contemplation will become disturbed if the intellect is busying itself with many words. She says that fire can be kindled by "a few little straws" laid down in humility, rather than from too many concepts from learned reasoning.

Effects of Contemplative Prayer

The prayer of quiet brings deep assurance of salvation, a desire to do penance for love of the Lord without fear of risking one's health, total courage in facing trials and tribulations, a great desire to do everything for God, the eyes to see the misery of our own human condition and that earthly things are as nothing as long as we have Christ, and it brings a strengthening of all the virtues.[113] However, Teresa warns about backsliding from this state of prayer. Anyone who has been given this gift and then falls back into serious sin may well collapse into a state worse than when they began the spiritual journey. The devil attacks people who have advanced to this stage in the spiritual life since their influence on others for good will be immense. They have potential for doing the devil much damage, so he will attack them more viciously than others in earlier states of the spiritual journey. She says "these souls suffer much combat, and if they go astray they stray much more than do others"[114]

The distinguishing feature of this sort of contemplative prayer, as it moves from recollection to the prayer of quiet is that the will becomes increasingly captive to the love of God. But the intellect and the imagination still remain somewhat unmanageable. Sometimes they will be quiet and give no trouble. At other times they will be out of control. She says that when the will is captured by the love of God "it shouldn't pay any more attention to the intellect than it would to a madman".[115] This is important to know, since in prayer we can become disturbed by the endless distractions of random thoughts and imaginings. When the mind runs away with crazy thoughts, don't follow it. Stay in the communion of love with the Lord. It is best to ignore the antics of the mind and the imagination. Teresa has two images to illustrate this point. From her own experience she describes the mind as "a mad woman" strapped to the blades of a wind-mill, screeching at the top of her voice as the blades revolve, but meanwhile the water is still being drawn up from the depths in quiet contemplation. In a more relational image she likens contemplation to friends conversing intimately while their children are over in a corner screaming for attention. The recalcitrant children represent the mind and the imagination. If the friends leave their conversation to deal with the children by trying to silence them, their communion is lost.

The Garden

In *The Book of Her Life* Teresa images the spiritual life as a garden with a well in the centre.[116] The aim is to draw up water from the well in order to help the garden grow. The garden has many flowers which are the virtues that need watering for them to grow. In the early stages of the spiritual life when we are still breaking with the world, struggling with overcoming flesh desires and beset by countless temptations, it is hard work to get the water up from the well and onto the garden. While we have a bucket with a rope tied to its handle we have to manually throw the bucket down to the water in the well then laboriously haul it up and carry it to the waiting flowers. This is the time when the usual way of prayer is discursive meditation, which requires much concentration and seems to be often full of distractions, dryness and desolation.

During this early time it is important to persevere in breaking with our previous sinful life and develop a virtuous way of life in imitation of Jesus. Self-denial in union with Jesus crucified is essential, and various testings will help develop humility, practical love and obedience in our lives. It is important to have a spiritual director who is prudent, experienced in the spiritual life and learned. As we begin to establish a life of genuine discipleship one of the great dangers is to settle for mediocrity. Rather than pressing on in a life with God, we are tempted to self-preservation. Having attained a certain level of transformation where we are not likely to fall anymore into serious sin, and are established in a regular ecclesial life, we decide this is good enough. But God is always calling for more. He does not want us going to him at a snail's pace. We should desire to be great in God. Teresa says, "In this matter of desires, I have always had great ones…". She believes God is "a friend of courageous souls". We are not to put limits on what God can do, because he is eager to do more things with us than we could imagine. She says we need to have humility before God, but this does not mean being timid about our spiritual growth. Rather we are to have a "holy daring", and it pleases God when we are not content with little, since he bestows his gifts according to the measure of our desire.

Teresa then, continuing with the image of the garden, describes the transition from meditation to contemplation. She is aware that during the meditative phase the prayer becomes more and more simple and affective, leading into the experience of recollection as described earlier. Then, by the grace of God, the gift of contemplation is bestowed. Now God provides a windlass so that the bucket can be drawn up from the well quickly and the flowers can be watered more assuredly. With the prayer of passive recollection and the prayer of quiet the will becomes captive to the Lord in love, and there is a stillness of peace and joy in the heart. The prayer is now effortless and bears much more fruit in the garden of one's life. It brings supernatural consolation, a spiritual delight which has no sensuality about it, and the soul loses any covetousness for the things of the earth.

Teresa goes on to describe a garden which now has a river running through it which irrigates the garden even more effectively. This is what she calls the prayer of union which follows on from the prayer of quiet. I don't intend to linger on this since it is beyond the experience of most, but it involves the intellect and imagination, indeed all the faculties, being caught up in God in the experience she calls rapture. A final stage is when the garden is watered by constant rain, and this she identifies with the spiritual marriage. I want to emphasise that I don't think Teresa saw these stages, which she spells out more clearly in the *Interior Castle,* as a linear progression from one to the other as if they are exclusive to themselves. I tend to think that while the thrust forward is as she has described, we could find that while in recollection we may experience something of the prayer of quiet briefly. Or while in the prayer of quiet we may have a moment more akin to union. Most of all we should avoid trying to work out how our prayer is progressing. This is a fundamental trap. Self-analysis is not prayer. Worrying about our spiritual progress is a function of our self-love. It is simply a matter of continuing to focus on the Beloved. Rather than fall into introspection we need to open up our broken hearts to the One who knows us best and loves us most.

Experience of Renewal

The experience of the Charismatic Renewal has led me to conclude that often God gives a new outpouring of the Holy Spirit when people are at a very early stage in their spiritual journey. The purpose of the Spirit's coming is to bring about personal transformation. From the moment of receiving this "big grace" people sometimes experience directly the supernatural gift of the prayer of quiet, or at least the prayer of recollection. Having received this gift so suddenly, the challenge for them is to cooperate with the Holy Spirit who comes to sanctify. They need to engage fully in the work of breaking with sin, the devil, the world and the flesh, and work at growing in virtue. Unless they use the grace of contemplative prayer to go through this personal transformation by a disciplined way of life, all will be lost. Unfortunately, our experience has shown this to be true. On the other hand, if they remain faithful to the grace, and water the garden well, they will advance quickly in the spiritual life and God's purpose will be fulfilled not only in their personal sanctification, but also in increased missionary fervour for the Church.

In the writings of Teresa, and generally in the spiritual tradition since the Middle Ages, the usual expected progress in the spiritual life happens first with a prolonged time of purification during which the person learns self-denial and the spiritual disciplines, while working hard at discursive meditative prayer. This is classically called the purgative stage of the journey and at this time any experience of consolations and revelations would be viewed with some suspicion. In this scheme, the soul needs to prepare itself for the awakening to contemplation by detaching itself of all that is not of God so it can be emptied to receive eventually the infilling of the Spirit.

Sober Intoxication of the Spirit

What then to make of the contemporary experience of the new Pentecost which we call the "baptism in the Spirit"? Raniero Cantalamessa, preacher to the Papal household, calls this experience the "sober intoxication of the Spirit", and shows how various early Fathers of the Church give testimony to it as normal part of their sacramental initiation into the life of the Church.[117] Origin, Ambrose of Milan, Cyril of Jerusalem and others, identify the Pentecost experience of the Holy Spirit by the apostles as a "spiritual intoxication" given directly by God for their sanctification and mission. They expected this big grace to be bestowed by the Lord when neophytes were being initiated into the life of the Church. They draw upon Paul's language when writing to the Ephesians, "Do not get drunk with wine, for that is debauchery; but be filled with the Spirit, as you sing psalms and hymns and spiritual songs among yourselves, singing and making melody to the Lord in your hearts" (Eph 5:18-19).

According to the Fathers, rather than coming at the end of a long period of purification and formation as a disciple, the infusion of the Spirit is expected at the very beginning of the spiritual journey within the Church. This is also the current experience in the Charismatic Renewal. Ordinary lay people, in response to the preaching of the gospel, who have not been initiated into anything of the spiritual disciplines, can be opened up in their hearts to the infilling of the fire of God's love in a powerful and life-changing way. And as I mentioned earlier this new infilling is often accompanied with the first flowering of contemplation. I find this reality undeniable, even though some contemporary spiritual directors do not acknowledge this and fail to understand what is happening. Unfortunately, some can even dissuade people from the Renewal and discredit the experience as emotionalism or overzealous enthusiasm. In this they gravely mislead people and deprive them of the graces that God himself is bestowing.

I believe it is incumbent on those who prepare people to receive the baptism in the Spirit, that they realise the need for good training and pastoral care *after* the experience. This happens best in the context of a community of committed disciples. The main need of those who have received this holy intoxication is to have people around them who will help them to make sure it bears fruit in their life through personal purification and transformation. Because they have not had a long period of interior purgation prior to their conversion experience, they need to be led into the spiritual disciplines which will deepen them in a life in the Spirit. Otherwise all that has been gained by God's gracious anointing in the Spirit can be lost. But the immense advantage of this "sober intoxication in the Spirit" is that the boat of the neophyte is, as it were, provided with a sail, and in some cases even an in-built propeller, which powers them forward in a vigorous way and provides the zeal and courage for the journey ahead. A spiritual director who cannot see this would be a "blind guide" indeed.

Wise spiritual directors will draw alongside those who have experienced this "intoxication of the Spirit" and help them go through the hard work of self-discipline and embracing the Cross necessary for a sustained journey as a disciple of Jesus. It is my firm conviction that this big grace of "baptism in the Spirit" is meant, among other things, to bring all the baptised into the experience of contemplation.

FRANCIS DE SALES

Chronology
1567 - born in Chateau de Sales
1592 - a sign from God; his calling
1593 - ordained priest
1594 - mission to Chablais region
1602 - consecrated bishop at Thorens
1608 - Published *Introduction to the Devout Life*
1617 - Published *Treatise on the Love of God*
1622 - died on Dec 28 at Lyons

Quotes

Be patient with everyone, but above all with yourself...

do not be disheartened by your imperfections,

but always rise up with fresh courage.

Fits of anger, vexation, and bitterness against ourselves

tend to pride and they spring from no other source than self-love,

which is disturbed and upset at seeing that it is imperfect.

Certainly all virtues are very dear to God,

but humility pleases Him above all the others,

and it seems that He can refuse it nothing.

Never be in a hurry; do everything quietly and in a calm spirit. Do not lose your inner peace for anything whatsoever, even if your whole world seems upset.

FRANCIS DE SALES

Francis de Sales was born in 1567 at Thorens in Savoy, which was then independent from France. The region was bordered by Geneva, a Calvinist stronghold. This proximity to Geneva was to shape his future. Three years before Francis was born John Calvin died. For thirty years Calvin, a self-proclaimed reformist, had attempted to turn Geneva and the surrounding region into a perfect society free of immorality and corruption. His puritanical social engineering was based on a firm belief that Christ did not die on the Cross for all people, but only for the "elect". Only those destined from all eternity to be saved would gain heaven. The rest were destined to hell. Geneva was to be the city of God, the home of the elect. This harsh doctrine and its rigid moral consequences was still dominating the region as Francis was growing to manhood. It would later become the primary battle ground of his ministry as a priest.

Francis' parents were of noble descent and devout Catholics.[118] He was a frail child but highly intelligent. At the age of six he was enrolled in a prestigious boarding school not far from Thorens. Two years later he entered a school for sons of nobility in Annecy, Savoy. When he was eleven he asked his father's permission to be tonsured, being set apart for the clerical life. Reluctantly his father agreed, but he still harboured alternative ambitions for his promising son. Such a fine boy should be destined to carry on the family name and fortune in a law career! The next year Francis left for Paris to study humanities and philosophy at the Jesuit College of Clermont and gained his baccalaureate degree at the age of seventeen in 1584. He continued his post-graduate studies, but unknown to his father he was secretly studying theology at the Sorbonne. Already God was claiming his young heart.

Towards Priesthood

When he was nineteen Francis underwent a profound spiritual crisis. He was distressed that his teachers could not refute Calvin's doctrine of "double predestination". This teaching was at the heart of the Calvinists' heresy: that God predestines some people to heaven, but most are predestined to go to hell. They drew upon the writings of St Augustine to supposedly prove their case. His Dominican teachers were ill-equipped to dispute this false teaching. Being a sensitive soul, Francis fell into despair, anguishing over the growing conviction that, even though he loved God with all his heart, he was destined to eternal damnation in hell. Then one day while praying at the chapel of the Black Virgin in the Dominican Church of St Etienne du Gres, he made an act of total abandonment to God's will and vowed to serve him, regardless of whatever God had predestined for him. He then devoutly read the prayer which was written on a tablet hanging before him. It was the *Memorare*. From that moment he was totally free of his scruples and was filled with confidence and peace. Having been touched deeply by the love of God he abandoned totally any allegiance to the rigid Calvinist ideology. He now confidently embraced the merciful heart of God.

In 1588 at twenty one years of age he received his licentiate, which is the equivalent of a Masters in philosophy, and a Master of Arts. Now he was equipped to study law at the University of Padua. While dutifully keeping to his father's program his real interest lay elsewhere; he secretly kept reading the Fathers of the Church and theological works. In 1591 he received his doctorate in law and then returned to Savoy, where his father had purchased an estate for him, and arranged for him to become engaged to the beautiful daughter of the counsellor of the Duke of Savoy. Francis avoided his father's plan for his marriage, but agreed to be admitted to the bar at Chambery. Then on his return trip from the ceremony, even though he was a trained horseman, he was suddenly thrown from his horse. His sword fell out of his scabbard and together with the scabbard formed the sign of the cross on the ground. Picking himself up unharmed from the fall Francis was startled by the sign of the cross and interpreted it as divine confirmation of what had been in his heart for some time. He was meant to give himself to Christ as a priest.

To Francis' dismay on arriving home he discovered letters from the Duke naming him as a Senator. Francis flatly refused the honour, much to the chagrin of his father, who was adamantly opposed to the idea of priesthood for his promising son. But the hidden hand of God was at work to win over his father's opposition. Unknown to Francis he had been nominated from Rome to become the provost of the diocese, the second most important post to the bishop, even though he was not yet a priest. It was a great honour for the family. Not that Francis cared for the prestige, but it was enough for his father to finally concede defeat. All obstacles removed, the young man at twenty six years of age was ordained.

The Mission to Chablais

Almost immediately Francis was thrown into missionary activity. The Chablais region, an area about thirty miles long and fifteen miles wide, bordering on Savoy, had been won back under the rule of the Duke of Savoy. Of the 25,000 people living there only about 100 were Catholics. The others were convinced Calvinists. The Duke asked Francis' bishop to send priests to win back people to the Catholic faith. There were 50 parishes in the region, but the previous priests had been expelled. The bishop called an assembly of his priests and asked for volunteers. Francis and one other priest decided to take up the challenge. While living in a friendly Castle close to the Chablais region Francis would each day make the ten mile journey by foot into the hostile territory seeking to persuade the people. The opposition was intense. He was attacked by men wanting to kill him. Unprotected from the elements in winter snow he was once assailed by wolves and found refuge in a tree. He was mocked by Protestant ministers as a hypocrite, idolator and false prophet, relying on magic and sorcery and not the word of God. Francis endured the abuse, meeting it with gentleness and kindly persuasion. He used tracts, or pamphlets, placing them under the doors, or wherever they may be seen. By 1595 he was able to take up residence with a Catholic lady in Thonon, the capital of Chablais.

Gradually he was making inroads. His first convert, Pierre Poncet, was a famous lawyer, won over by Francis' conviction and his gentle manner. He began to win sympathy. Eventually he entered into the open market and would speak for two hours to the assembled crowd. Alarmed at his growing popularity Calvinist ministers challenged him to a public debate in the Town Hall. A large crowd gathered for the spectacle. But the Protestant ministers did not appear. The crowd was shocked. Francis had won the battle without a shot being fired. As a result the Baron d'Avully, who Francis had befriended over a year with many long conversations, finally abjured his heresy and confessed the Catholic faith. News of this conversion brought uproar in Geneva. One of their famous ministers was to come to Thonon to confront the turn-coat Baron d'Avully. But he delayed in coming. So Francis took the bull by the horns and declared that he and the newly converted Baron would come to Geneva! The confrontation in Geneva confirmed the Baron even more so in the Catholic faith.

That Christmas Francis bravely decided to celebrate three Masses in a church in Thonon. News of this outrage caused a great hullabaloo in the town, but Francis held firm against all opposition. Around the same time Francis was having clandestine visits with the great Calvinist theologian, Theodore de Beze, who was Calvin's successor in Geneva. Beze was later converted to the Catholic faith while he was listening to a sermon by Francis on the real presence of Christ in the Eucharist. It was in fact Eucharistic adoration which won many back to the Catholic faith. Francis and his growing number of supporters would celebrate Forty Hours devotion before the Blessed Sacrament which drew large crowds of people who in the cold, sterile world of Calvinism had been starved of the more tangible, warm and incarnational dimension of their Christian faith.

In 1602 Bishop de Granier of Savoy died and Francis was appointed to replace him. Francis was an affectionate, approachable, accessible bishop, equally popular amongst the poorest of the poor and the upper echelons of society. He led a simple lifestyle and had a frugal table. His reputation for holiness grew and his charismatic preaching was well known. With the publication of his two books, the *Introduction to the Devout Life* and the *Treatise on the Love of God*, he was widely sought as a teacher of the spiritual life. In 1619 when he was visiting Paris he had to climb a ladder and crawl through a window to reach the pulpit because the assembled crowds had packed every nook and cranny to hear him. It was said that people would weep just by looking at his face which radiated holiness, putting them in touch with the face of Christ.

In 1604 Francis had met Jane Frances de Chantal, a recently widowed mother of four children. She inspired in him a desire to found a new religious congregation dedicated to the care of the poor and the sick. Francis received a special revelation that she was to be the co-foundress, but she had to wait until she had her children off her hands. Ten years later Jane Frances arrived in Annecy to join Francis for the official foundation of the Sisters of the Visitation.

On The Love of God

Francis' book the *Introduction to the devout life*[119] was a popular bestseller throughout Europe, probably because, unlike most spiritual books of its time, it was not addressed primarily to priests and religious. The current mentality was that growth in holiness was the preserve of priests and religious, and if you had aspirations towards deepening in the love of God you were expected to take up that kind of vocation. Francis wrote for all Christians, recognising that every baptised person is called to holiness. He wanted to provide a guide for the spiritual life for all the baptised, no matter what their state of life. Those of us who have grown up in a post Vatican II Church do not find this proposition all that strange, but in Francis' world and even in the Catholic popular mind prior to the Second Vatican Council it was not widely accepted. This is the main reason why this volume still holds appeal today. It provides practical wisdom for anyone wishing to be a disciple of Jesus Christ.

At the very beginning of the *Introduction* Francis enunciates his first principle, which in fact is the foundation of all his teaching.[120] He asks the question: how do we know what constitutes a "devout life"? Or, put another way, what is the basis for true holiness? How does one become holy? There are many states of life and each of them can be a way of holiness, but what is fundamental for anyone to be holy? He says some may seek "true devotion" by long and gruelling fasts and extended periods of abstinence. Others may say holiness is about long hours in prayer and lots of devotional exercises. Yet others may say the real criterion of holiness is generosity in almsgiving. We may even think that to be holy is to engage in endless pious acts, to dress ceremoniously in a religious fashion, and to engage in exotic ascetical practices. But in fact, holiness is about the love of God in action. It may involve many of the activities mentioned, but if it is not motivated by the love of God it is not genuine holiness.

Francis is very aware that the love of God is a gift; not something we can stir up by our own energetic desire and will power. In his classic work entitled *Treatise on the Love of God* he makes it clear that human beings are designed to love God with our whole heart, soul, mind and strength, and also to love our neighbour. But these two loves cannot be engendered by ourselves alone but only by God's grace. Religion goes wrong when people are trying earnestly to win God's favour through their good works without first realising that God loves them regardless of what they do or don't do. Nothing we perform or don't perform can change the reality of God's love for us. As I have stated elsewhere:

> The starting point for the spiritual life and the means to all growth is the experience of God's love. It is totally unmerited gift from God. His love for us is completely unconditional and has no limits. The single most important thing in anyone's life is to encounter this love. To become holy involves many steps, but underneath it all is simply letting God love you, and responding wholeheartedly and unconditionally to this love.[121]

No matter how pious we are or how eager to grow in perfection, we cannot earn God's love by striving to be good. Our religious practices become a spiritual treadmill, asserting much effort but going nowhere. We can try by many methods to climb the ladder of perfection, but keep falling off and becoming distraught about our fragility. But this is starting the journey the wrong way around. John, the beloved disciple, sets us right when he says: "This is the love I mean: not our love for God, but God's love for us when he sent his Son to be the sacrifice that takes our sins away" (1John 4:10). What matters is that God has first loved us.

Grace Draws the Heart

One of Francis de Sales' best contributions is his understanding of grace which he gives in his *Treatise on the Love of God*. He describes how God loves us so much that he does not force his way into our lives or demand things by overriding our free will. Rather he seeks to win us by his love, thus drawing our hearts into union with him. He has come to convince us of his love by his death on the Cross for us. As Paul says, "What proves that God loves us is that Christ died for us" (Rom 5:8). The fall of the human race in Adam did not turn God against us in anger, but instead stimulated his love even more. This is the meaning of the words in the Easter Exultet: "O happy fault, O necessary sin of Adam, which gained for us so great a Redeemer". Our loss due to our sin actually proved to be our gain! We have received more grace through being redeemed by our Saviour than we would ever have received from Adam's unsullied innocence.[122]

When we look to Jesus, our Saviour, on the Cross we see his blood shed as a ransom for us, a clear demonstration of his infinite longing for us to love him.[123] He cried out "I have come to bring fire to the earth, and how I long for this to happen already" (Lk 12:49). This longing in the heart of Jesus is for union with each one of us, that we would know the fire of love that was within him as he went to the Cross, and which he intended to be cast upon us in the Pentecost experience. At the Last Supper Jesus says, "I have longed with a great longing to share this meal with you" (Lk 22:15). His desire for union with us is total; he went to the extreme of giving everything for us, because as Francis says, "love seeks union".

Paul says: "The love of Christ overwhelms us when we reflect that if one man died for all, then all should be dead" (2Cor 5:14). We become persuaded by his love, we are won over by it, and we find ourselves surrendering to it with a whole-hearted response. Francis is keen to have us understand that God leaves us free: "Grace lays hold of the heart in such a way as not to impair free will".[124] But grace is the persuasion of God's love. Like iron filings attracted to a magnet so are our hearts attracted by his love. But unlike the iron filings we are free to respond or to reject his love. "Grace", he says "is powerful, not to compel the heart, but to allure it; grace is vehement, not to outrage our liberty, but to fill it with love; grace is intensely active – but so gently it does not override the will; grace exerts influence on us – but does not suppress our freedom"[125].

God's Desire Awakens Our Desire

Grace acts much like a lover wooing his beloved, helping her to believe that she is lovable, and awaking love within her. God's desire for union with us creates an insatiable desire within us for union with him. He thirsts for us in the way that Jesus asked the woman at the well for a drink. Even though she protested he said, "If only you knew what God is offering and who it is that is saying to you: Give me a drink, you would have been the one to ask, and he would have given you living water… the water that I shall give will turn into a spring inside of you, welling up to eternal life" (Jn 4:10-14). His thirst for her soul awakens a thirst in her heart and she is promised a spring of living water breaking forth in the depth of her being.

All is God's grace. Francis says that the first grace attracting the heart, prevenient grace, by which God prompts and awakens us, happens without our cooperation. We are often not even aware of this grace at work preparing the ground for a decision of the will. All further graces that come to us from God require our consent, and our cooperation.[126] The Lord's loving attractions overwhelm us and lead us to deeper faith and love. The Lord is generous with many inspirations, seeking to persuade our hearts and win us to him. If we allow his advances, our will falls captive to his allurements. It is so wonderful to be loved by God.

We can say with certainty that the single most important thing in the spiritual life is to allow oneself to be loved by God and hold no obstacle before him. Even when we do place a barrier to his love he will still press in towards us as Jesus did to Peter when he had denied that he even knew him. Peter repented after he saw the gentle merciful eyes of Jesus, and with the gift of compunction, shedding many tears, he was restored to union with the Lord.[127] Jesus wants us to experience him as our intimate friend. He told us, "I do not call you servants anymore since a servant does not know his master's business. I call you friends if you do what I command you" (Jn 15:15). Jesus is always talking to us by "constant inspirations, attractions, impulses of grace". He wants to share the secrets of his Father's heart with us as a friend does. Even when we let him down, like Peter, he does not give up on us, but waits for our return.

Gratifying Love

Another important contribution of Francis de Sales is in the way he describes growth in the love of God. He says that the initial passionate love for the Lord becomes purified so the soul ultimately just wants what pleases the Lord. This will happen over time. Our love for God will at first be what he calls "gratifying" love, and then later it will have added to it "benevolent" or "disinterested" love. Gratifying love is when we feel the pleasure of God's delight, and this brings deep satisfaction. Francis does not mean a selfish love which is just about one's own gain. Rather, the Holy Spirit has poured the love of God into our heart, and our will is galvanised in passionate love for our Beloved. We find our rest in God and feed on his delights.[128] It is the experience of being like a child in its mother's arms, joyfully allowing oneself to be embraced by the immense love of God. Just like a mother with her child, God woos and wins the soul[129]. In response we long for more of his love. We cannot have enough of his goodness. This longing for God is an unceasing desire for union with him. While we are gratified by his love, we still are hungry for more. We feel deep within the core of our being that we possess God as our prized lover, and we also feel possessed by him. We find him imprinting his very likeness on us; consequently his qualities begin to become evident in our life. Francis quotes Augustine: "The lover is always seeking his beloved; love goes on seeking what it has already found —not to have it, but to have it always".[130]

In a beautiful passage on Mary's experience of the passion of Jesus Francis illustrates how gratifying love arises from empathy with the beloved.[131] By this gift of empathy or compassion we "feel with" the one whom we love.

> Above all, think how love carved all our Redeemer's grief, torture, fatigue, pain, anguish, wounds, his whole passion and death, on the heart of his blessed Mother! Those nails which crucified the Son's body also crucified a Mother's heart; those thorns which pierced his brow pierced through into her devoted soul. She experienced her Son's distress by commiseration, his anguish by empathy, his sufferings by compassion: finally the sword of death which pierced that beloved Son's heart also transfixed the heart of his loving Mother.[132]

This passage reminds us of the words of the *Stabat Mater*: "Holy Mother pierce me through, in my heart each wound renew of my Saviour crucified". It is an invitation to walk with Mary through the passion of Jesus unto Calvary, inviting her to take us into "being with Jesus", feeling within our own hearts the agony of Jesus. We feel a loving empathy with Jesus as the nails are belted into his hands and feet, as the Cross is roughly raised with his body fastened to it, and as he endures three hours of excruciatingly painful torture, and finally as he is slowly asphyxiated. But it is not the horrendous physical suffering that moves us most, even though it makes us shudder with horror. Rather it is the unconditional love by which he suffered which wins our heart, and calls forth a response of passionate love for him who died for us.

> Unbearable are the torments he suffers, this divine lover of mine: that is what grieves me, leaves me senseless with pain. Yet he is glad to suffer; he welcomes the agony; death is joy to him, because all its pains are for me. That is why, saddened as I am by his sufferings, I am beside myself with joy at his love; not only do I grieve him, I also boast of him.[133]

Benevolent Love

God's purpose is to refine our love. While we retain this "gratifying" kind of love, we begin to want to love God for his own sake, and we want to return to God something for his goodness to us. However, there is nothing that we have to give God, except our wills. Hence, the emergence of "benevolent" love, which simply wants to praise the Lord for who he is, and to see him glorified always. "Benevolent" love wants only to do the Lord's will; simply to please him at all costs. When benevolent love kicks in, we delight in him for no other reason than he is God. We want to extol him, praise him, and the words of the *Our Father* become more intentional: "Hallowed be thy name". We feel our efforts to praise him fall pitifully short of his grandeur and this stirs us to want to praise him beyond any limits. We praise him not for any personal gain, but simply because he is worthy of praise.

Francis says that both these kinds of love are part of our journey to God. "Gratifying" love provides the passionate fire of the saints. But for this to happen it has to become purified, and complemented by "benevolent" love. As we become more intent on simply pleasing God and doing anything we can for him, we seek "gratification" not for the delight it gives us, but for the delight it gives to God. The movement is toward total submission to the will of God in all circumstances. Francis says, "This is the way, then, in which the heart of man grows in likeness to the heart of God – when benevolent love causes us to leave our hearts in God's hands, to be moulded to his will, fashioned to his liking."[134]

Francis also calls this "disinterested love". He says:

> The heart of a disinterested man is like wax in God's hands, ready for every impression of the eternal will. Such a heart knows no personal preference, equally prepared for anything, its one aim is to fulfil God's will…It comes to this: the goal which the disinterested man has most at heart is simply to please God.[135]

For The King's Pleasure

Francis tells a story of a fine musician, a marvellous lute player, who suddenly went stone deaf. The lute-player kept his skill, which he had developed over years. He loved to play the lute for the King who was a childhood friend of his. Even though the lute player could not gain any pleasure from hearing his music, he was still delighted to see the King's pleasure when he played. But one day the King commanded the lute-player to continue playing, because the music was pleasing to the King, but the King went out hunting! So now the lute-player was to play out of love for the King, and not even have the satisfaction of the King's presence and seeing the King's delight. For the lute-player there was "nothing in it for him anymore", except the knowledge that brought profound peace that he was doing what the King desired.

As we develop more in this "benevolent" love, we do not judge our prayer time on the degree of pleasure we had, or the amount of enlightenment we were given, or the inspirations or images that came our way, or any other gift from God. We simply judge it by whether or not we were faithful and generous during the time of prayer. That is, no matter what transpired, we did not give up, but persevered in playing the song for the King; and we were generous in doing so.

God allows times of dryness or desolation during our times of prayer so that we will get more in touch with our weakness and utter dependency on him. He wants us to love him for his own sake, not just for the gifts he bestows. When at prayer our thoughts should not be on ourselves, or how the experience is going or what we are getting out of the experience. Rather, we are there for God alone, and being with him is enough consolation since that is what really pleases him. Francis makes an observation:

> Look at that man over there, saying his prayers... he seems to be so devoted, so on fire with love. Wait a while, however, and you will see if it is really God he loves. As soon as the charm and gratification which he feels in loving end, as soon as dryness appears, he will not keep up, but only pray occasionally. Had it been God he was loving, why did he stop? After all, God is still God. It was the consolation that God gives that he was in love with, not the God who gives all consolation.[136]

Gentleness

The quality that shines most clearly in the life of Francis de Sales is gentleness of heart. Having, as a young man, been rescued by the Virgin Mary from the despairing thoughts of being numbered among the damned, he was filled with the gentle, loving mercy of God. His whole world-view and outlook on life in general was coloured by this primary experience of the tender merciful heart of God. Rather than succumb to the cold harsh punitive God of the Calvinists he opened his heart to the warm gentle accepting heart of God as revealed in the Scriptures. His attitude towards others was characterized by this gentleness. We have seen how he persuaded Calvinists in the Chablais region to return to the faith through speaking to them with friendship and respect rather than with accusation and condemnation. He engaged in disputation but in a kind and respectful manner. He won people by his gentleness.

He counsels us never to let the sun go down on our anger. If we are stung by slander or some false accusation it is not for us to swell up in vengeful thinking or irate outbursts. Rather we are to meet it with gentleness and humility. When anger rises to stir up a storm in the heart we are to cry out to God for help. Just as Jesus stilled the waters of Galilee he is sure to say, "Peace, be still". If we do happen to break out in rage then we should make amends by immediately following it with an act of meekness. To move in the opposite spirit takes the sting out the rage and deflates its power.

Francis counsels also being gentle with ourselves or with our imperfections and failings. We can be too hard on ourselves, falling into self-recrimination and self-hate which is very destructive. He warns that "all this anger and irritation against one's self fosters pride and springs entirely from self-love, which is disturbed and fretted by its own imperfections".[137] It is useless and counterproductive to keep blaming ourselves for our failures. This causes us to lose heart altogether. With all our many imperfections we must trust in the tender loving mercy of God:

> So then, when you have fallen, lift up your heart in quietness, humbling yourself deeply before God by reason of your frailty, without being amazed that you fell; there is no cause to marvel because weakness is weak and infirmity infirm. With all your heart lament that you should have offended God, and begin to cultivate again the grace that was lost, with a very deep trust in His Mercy, and with a bold, brave heart.[138]

Accepting Failure

One of the biggest obstacles to growth in the spiritual life is becoming anxious about your seeming failure to grow. Francis says:

> This unresting anxiety is the greatest evil which can happen to the soul, sin only excepted. Just as internal disruptions ruin a country, so if your heart be disturbed and anxious, it loses power to retain such graces as it has, as well as strength to resist temptations of the Evil One, who is all the more ready to fish in troubled waters.[139]

If we get impatient and troubled about our spiritual growth this anxiety begets further anxiety, leading to greater distress for the soul. If we are striving to overcome a particular sinful pattern the worst thing is to become anxious about it. Rather keep a calm restful spirit and steadily work towards the goal without being too worried about occasional falls. The main principle in the spiritual life is not to whip yourself about failure, but when the fall occurs, quickly and gently pick yourself up, be sorrowful of heart before the Lord, repent by a decision of the will, and then continue on the journey without any further recriminations.

Overcoming Anxiety

Francis was aware that anxiety is fed by negative thoughts, envisaging the worst case scenario, and in a twisted way almost willing the worst to happen.[140] He counsels that if the mind starts moving in that direction dispute the thoughts with the truth and do not let the tendency to "catastrophise" rule the heart. Jesus said, "If you make my word your home you will indeed be my disciples, you will learn the truth, and the truth will set you free" (Jn 8:31-32). Francis gives an early version of what we now know as cognitive behavioural therapy. We need to identify the "stinking thinking" which arises from false core beliefs, and instead of succumbing to these lies re-program our minds with the truth. He also says it is good to occupy oneself with external works and sport, and divert the mind from thoughts that would sabotage the soul, putting in their place good and cheerful thoughts. He encourages holding on to the crucifix, kissing it, and putting our trust in the loving mercy of our Saviour. It is important to lay bare everything before a confessor and spiritual director. And we would add, of course, if necessary, a trained counsellor.

In today's world tensions and anxieties seem epidemic. They are the underlying cause of many medical problems – ulcers, heart attacks, migraines, intestinal issues and skin diseases. People looking for peace turn to many solutions – dietary supplements, yoga, transcendental meditation, massages, hypnosis, or simply overdosing on alcohol, pills or drugs. None of these can provide the peace our heart is so desperately seeking. Francis would point us towards Jesus, who promises, "I will give you a peace that the world cannot understand. I give you a peace that no one can take from you" (Jn 14:27). We can rest easy in our hearts when we know that everything is in the hands of the Lord. No situation is outside his control. He is watching over us, with his angels around us (Ps 91:11). Every hair on our head is counted by him. We can surrender all anxious situations into his hands. "Cast all your cares upon the Lord, for he is looking after you" (1Pet 5:7). When we open up our hearts to his love, the anxiety dissolves: "His perfect love drives out all fear" (1 John 4:18).

MARGARET MARY ALOCOQUE

Chronology

1647 - born in Verosvres, France
1671 - enters Convent of Visitation in Paray-le-Monial
1673 - first apparition of the Heart of Jesus
1674 - second apparition of the Heart of Jesus
1675 - third apparition of the Heart of Jesus
1686 - first public devotion to the Sacred Heart
1690 - dies on 17 October in Paray-le-Monial

Quotes

The sacred heart of Christ is an inexhaustible fountain and its sole desire is to pour itself out into the hearts of the humble so as to free them and prepare them to lead lives according to his good pleasure.

Go courageously to God, along the way He has traced out for you, steadfastly embracing the means He offers you.

We must not belong to God by halves; as God gives himself entirely to the soul he loves, so does he desire to possess the soul's entire love.

Our heart is made for God. Woe, then, if it
be satisfied with less than God,
or if it allow itself to burn with any other fire
than that of his pure love.

MARGARET MARY ALACOQUE

I am including Margaret Mary in this list of influential saints because she was the chosen instrument of the Lord to receive the revelations of the heart of Jesus. Given her humble self-effacing life I have no doubt she would be delighted not to be the central focus of these reflections. Rather she would want the loving heart of Jesus to seize our attention and call forth a whole-hearted response from us.

Fifty years after the death of Francis de Sales in a small convent of the Visitation Sisters in Paray-le-Monial Margaret Mary at the age of twenty six years had three major apparitions over a period of a few months which were destined to have universal impact on the whole Catholic world. When Francis had founded the Visitation sisters he chose for their insignia a single heart pierced by two arrows, symbolising the pierced heart of Jesus and Mary, set in a crown of thorns, forming the base of a cross on which was inscribed the names of Jesus and Mary. Imparting this image to Jane Francis de Chantal he said, "Our little congregation is the work of the hearts of Jesus and Mary. By opening his sacred heart, the dying Saviour brought us to birth".[141] Francis had predicted "this humble little Institute will be blessed beyond all human calculation." And so it was. Through the revelations given to a humble, self-effacing, fiercely ascetical young sister who lived for love of God alone, the prophecy of Francis was realised way beyond what even he could have imagined.

True Meaning of the Devotion

Before reflecting on Margaret Mary's apparitions we need to put these private revelations of the heart of Jesus in a broader context. The devotion to the heart of Jesus was not just a seventeenth century phenomenon. Unfortunately, its popular devotion in the

Church since Margaret Mary has often degenerated into pietistic, sentimentality, robbing it of its truly strong and robust character. We need to recapture its scriptural and patristic foundation and trace its history prior to its final flowering with Margaret Mary.[142] The "heart" in scripture refers to the inner core of a person; the centre of all thoughts, feelings, attitudes, emotions, imagination, memories; all actions flow from the heart. Love for the heart of Jesus then is love for his humanity. Devotion to the heart of Jesus is not a relationship with a physical organ of the heart. The physical organ is just a symbol of the love that burns in the depths of Christ's humanity. We reverence the divine love in the human heart of Jesus for us. "Deep calls upon deep in the roar of mighty cataracts" (Ps 42:8). The divine love in the human heart of Jesus is calling forth a response of love in our hearts and a deep desire for the conversion of the world to his heart.

Scriptural Themes

There are three major scriptural themes which the Fathers of the Church drew upon to focus attention on the heart of Jesus. Firstly, the wounds of Jesus, especially the side of Jesus on the Cross opened up by the lance from which flowed blood and water. The Church, the new Eve, was born from the side of Christ, as once Eve was brought from the side of Adam. The blood and water symbolised, the pouring of water at baptism and gift of Eucharist. The wounded heart of Jesus on the Cross was the source of sacramental life for the Church. Secondly, they remembered John the Beloved reclining on the chest of Jesus at the Last Supper – resting close to the fountain of life, enjoying quiet contemplation in heart to heart love with the Saviour. This theme has been carried through until our present day as a symbol of intimacy with Jesus; listening to his heartbeat, and drawing from his tender, merciful love for us. Jesus had said, "Come to me all you who labour and are heavy burdened, and I will give you rest. Take up my yoke from me and learn from me, for I am gentle and humble of heart. And you will have rest for your souls" (Matthew 11:28-30).

The third scriptural theme used often by the Fathers is the romantic language of heartfelt love in the Song of Songs. For example, Gregory the Great voices the invitation of Jesus to his beloved using nuptial imagery:

> Arise, my love, my sister, and come, my dove, in the depths of the rock, in the hollow places in the wall. By the clefts of the rock I mean the wounds in my hands and my feet hanging freely on the cross. By the hollow places in the wall I mean the wound in my side made by the lance. Like the dove in the rock the simple soul finds in the wounds the food that will strengthen her. (cf Song 2:13-14)

The Heart of God

The Old Testament covenantal notion of the "heart of God" of all tenderness, fidelity, love, goodness, kindness and mercy finds its completion in New Testament revelation of the heart of Jesus. God's loving heart is now found manifest in the humanity of Jesus. The texts are manifold. But just to mention a few:

> But now thus says the Lord, who created you Jacob, who formed you, Israel: do not be afraid for I have redeemed you; I have called you by name, you are mine....You are precious in my eyes, because you are honoured and I love you. (Is 43:1-4)

> Does a woman forget the child at her breast or fail to cherish the son of her womb? But even if these forget I will never forget you. (Is 49:15)

> I myself taught Ephraim to walk, I took them in my arms; yet

> they have not understood I was the one looking after them. I led them with leading strings of love. I was like someone who lifts up an infant close against his cheek; stooping down to him I gave him his food. (Hos 11:3-4)
>
> I have loved you with an everlasting love and I am constant in my affection for you. (Jer 31:3)

Jesus came to bring us into relationship with the Father of all tenderness, mercy and love. "No one has ever seen God; it is only the Son, who is nearest to the Father's heart, who has made him known" (John 1:18). Jesus draws us into his own "heart to heart" experience of the Father, the eternal mutual love in the Trinity. At the Last Supper Jesus prays to the Father "that the love with which you love me may be in them, and so that I may be in them" (Jn 17:26). We are meant to share in the same intimacy Jesus has with the Father.

A Love that Embraces the World

From our communion with the heart of God, manifest in the human heart of Jesus, our hearts are expanded in love to embrace the whole world. The fruit of abiding in the heart of Jesus is love for one another, and love for the poor, broken, alienated and marginalised. It would be a lie to say that we love God whom we cannot see, while being indifferent to the brother or sister we can see. The proof of our love of God will be in our love for others (1Jn 4:20).

In this devotion we discover the heart of Jesus for the salvation of all men and women. We feel the wrenching in the heart of Jesus as he looked upon the crowds that were "harassed and dejected like sheep without a shepherd" (Mt 9:36). His thirst for souls becomes our thirst (cf Jn 19:28).

Gazing upon Jesus crucified we also become acutely aware of

our complicity in the sin of the world which nailed him there: "They shall look upon him whom they have pierced" (Jn 19:37). We now want to make up to Jesus for the lukewarm and lethargic way we have responded to his love. We find a new zeal for his kingdom.

Fountain From the Side of Christ

As I said earlier devotion to the heart of Jesus did not originate with the private revelations of Margaret Mary. The earliest Christians contemplated the crucified Christ with deep love. They focussed on veneration of his five wounds, but gradually the focus shifted to his wounded side opened for our salvation, from which flowed a fountain of living water for the life of the Church. Pius XII in an encyclical on the heart of Jesus clearly identifies the origin of the devotion from earliest years. He points out that gazing upon Jesus crucified and devotion to his holy wounds began very early in the life of the church:

> It must not be said that this devotion has taken its origin from some private revelation of God and has suddenly appeared in the church; rather, it has blossomed forth of its own accord as a result of that lively faith and burning devotion of men who were drawn towards the adorable Redeemer and his glorious wounds which they saw as irresistible proofs of that unbounded love.[143]

The early history of the devotion focussed on the phrase from John's gospel: "From his heart shall flow fountains of living water" (Jn 7:38), which was seen as a prophecy of a fountain of the life-giving Spirit flowing from the opened side of Jesus on the Cross (Jn 19:33-38). For example, St Irenaeus of Lyons says that we are meant to "drink from the crystal spring which flows from the body of Christ". In another place he states: "as the rock gave forth water to drink to the thirsty Israelites in the desert, the Rock which was Christ Jesus now gives to believers to drink the spiritual waters which lead to eternal life";[144] and again "Christ suffers and gives life. He is fastened with nails and yet is the source of the living waters. This water is the Spirit".[145] St Ambrose of Milan says, "Drink of Christ, for he is the fountain of life. Drink of Christ, for he is the stream whose torrents brought joy to the City of God. Drink of Christ for he is peace. Drink of Christ for the streams of living water flow from his bosom".[146]

Meditation of the Saints

In the Middle Ages holy men and women contemplated more intensely the passion of Jesus and his agony on the Cross not only being with him in his physical suffering, but also empathising with his interior anguish of heart. They looked towards his wounds as radiant signs of his love, and his heart as pierced through love for our sake. As Francis of Assisi and Dominic Guzman and their followers dwelt upon the passion and death of Jesus they focussed on this suffering heart of love. He was dying to show the depth of his love for us, and to win us by his love. By meditating on the Cross they experienced themselves being drawn into the wounded heart of Jesus, broken open in love for the world. We find this as well in Bonaventure, Albert the Great, Mechthild of Madeburg and Gertrude the Great, Catherine of Siena and Bridget of Sweden and so many others. By the time of the spiritual movement of *Devotio Moderna*[147] it was popular spiritual parlance. Thomas a Kempis author of the *Imitation of Christ* writes fervently of the heart of Jesus:

> Enter then, enter my soul into the right side of your crucified Lord, pass through the holy wound into the most loving heart of Jesus, which out of love was pierced by the lance, that you may rest in the clefts of the Rock (Song 2:14) from the trouble of the world. Enter then into the worshipful heart, to the hidden heart, to

the silent heart, to the heart of God which opens to you its portals ... Do draw from the side of Jesus sweet consolations for life, that you may no longer live to yourself, but in him who was wounded for you. Give him your heart who opens his heart to you.[148]

Not surprisingly many early Jesuits, particularly Peter Canisius, fostered this spirituality as well, continuing the work done by Fr Claude de la Colombiere (1641-1682), a holy and brilliant young Jesuit, who was Margaret Mary's God-given Jesuit spiritual director.

As we have already seen Francis de Sales' whole spirituality was permeated with the mystery of the heart of Jesus. In his *Treatise on the Love of God*, like Ignatius Loyola and Teresa of Avila upon whom he depends, he is clear that the way to God is the way he came to us, that is through the humanity of Jesus. All good spirituality will not bypass the humanity of Jesus, but will find this the sure path to the fullness of the love of God:

> The heart of Christ is the throne of God's love; of that we can be certain. Through the cleft in his pierced side the Saviour's love watches over the hearts of human kind; king of all hearts he is, so his eyes are on them always. The love of God's heart, or rather the heart of God's love – like someone looking through a lattice – has clear sight of our hearts, gazes on them lovingly; our view of it, however, is indistinct, something of which we catch only glimpses. Could we but once hear the divine praises as they pour from his sacred heart - only think of the joy we should know, only think how our hearts would leap heavenwards, to hear that praise forever![149]

The Apparitions

Francis de Sales had breathed his spirit into the foundation of the Sisters of the Visitation. Consequently, young Margaret Mary, having joined the Sisters against her mother's will on 20 June 1671, was praying within fertile ground when she was captivated by visions which crystallised and completed the spiritual tradition preceding her. Only two years after entering the convent this simple humble soul experienced her first vision on 27 December 1673.[150] While praying before the Blessed Sacrament she felt enveloped by God's presence: "I forgot all about myself, and where I was, it was so intense; I simply gave myself up to the Spirit of God - my heart a willing prey to the violence of his love". She experienced herself as leaning on the breast of Jesus, while he whispered to her the secrets of his heart. She felt "he opened his heart to me" in a way that she could not doubt. She heard him say:

> My divine heart is so passionately fond of the human race, and of you in particular, that it cannot keep back the pent-up flames of its burning love any longer. They must burst out through you and reveal my heart to the world, so as to enrich mankind with my precious treasures. I'm letting you see them now; and they include all the graces of sanctification needed to snatch men from the very brink of hell. You are the one I have chosen for this great scheme —you're so utterly unworthy and ignorant, it will be all my work.[151]

Then Jesus asked her for her heart. She begged him to take it. He placed it in his own divine heart. "He let me see it there – a tiny atom being completely burned up in that fiery furnace. Then he lifted it up and put it back where he had found it". He promised her that her heart would now burn with love relentlessly. She would know the pain of his own heart, burning with self-sacrificing love. He told her this gift is a "proof of my love for you, hiding in your side"; the intense heat she experienced from her heart aflame for God would never diminish. She said that for several days afterwards she felt "as though I was on fire and intoxicated"; on fire with love for the suffering Christ. On the first Friday of each month she received special graces along with the burning pain in her side, which she would not trade for anything.

The next revelation occurred in 1674, but the exact date is unknown. Here is her account of this second vision:

> The Blessed Sacrament was exposed, and I was experiencing an unusually complete state of recollection, my sense and faculties utterly withdrawn from their surroundings, when Jesus Christ, my kind Master, appeared to me. He was a blaze of glory – his five wounds shining like five suns, flames issuing from all parts of his human form, especially from his divine breast which was like a furnace, and which he opened to disclose his utterly affectionate and lovable heart, the living source of all those flames. It was at that moment that he revealed to me the indescribable wonders of his pure love for mankind: the extravagance to which he'd been led for those who had nothing for him but ingratitude and indifference.[152]

Jesus continued to reveal to her how much he continues to suffer because people ignore and reject his love for them. He asked Margaret Mary to make reparation for this ingratitude. She pointed out her inadequacy for the task. But he replied that "being here" was enough and seared into her soul a flame of love which she thought would devour her. She begged him to take pity on her weakness. He assured her of his support and told her not to be afraid. He then instructed her on what she was to do. She was to receive him in Holy Communion as often as possible, and to accept any mortification and humiliation as signs of his love. Every Thursday night she was to experience with him the agony in the garden of Gethsemane as she lay prostrate between eleven o'clock and midnight. This was to plead for mercy for sinners, and to soothe the heartache he felt when the apostles abandoned him. And during this hour she was to do whatever he would ask her.

Not long after this Margaret Mary obtained Fr Colombiere as her spiritual director, who guided her from that point onwards. Jesus had promised during the apparition that he would send her "my faithful servant and perfect friend" to help her. She poured out her soul to Fr Colombiere, and he strengthened her in preparation for the third major apparition in June 1675:

> One day, kneeling before the Blessed Sacrament during the octave of Corpus Christi, I was deluged with God's loving favours. Inspired to make some return, and to give him love for love, I heard him say: "Do what I've already so often asked you; you can't show your love in a finer way than that! He disclosed his heart as he spoke: 'There it is, that heart so deeply in love with men, it spared no means of proof - wearing itself out until it was utterly spent! This meets with scant appreciation from most of them; all I get back is ingratitude – witness their irreverence, their sacrileges, their coldness and contempt for me in this Sacrament of Love. What hurts me most is that hearts dedicated to my service behave in this way.[153]

The Lord went on to ask her to have the Friday after the octave of Corpus Christi set apart as a special feast in honour of his heart – a day on which to receive him in Holy Communion and make a solemn act of reparation for the indignities he has received in the Blessed Sacrament while exposed on the altars of the world. He said: "I promise you I shall open my heart to all who honour me in this way, and who get others to do the same; they will feel in all its fullness the power of my love".

For ten years Margaret Mary endured belittling humiliation from her fellow sisters, even though some of them tended to believe hesitatingly her account of the apparitions. Fr Colombiere was her constant and reliable spiritual support. But it was only two years after his death in 1684 that the community formally celebrated the feast of the Sacred Heart on 21 June 1686. The change in attitude came about when Fr Colombiere's retreat notes were published posthumously in Lyons. In these writings he spoke of a highly favoured soul who he knew personally, endorsed all the apparitions, and made it clear that he had no doubt that God had commissioned her to spread devotion to the Sacred Heart. With the backing of such a holy, authoritative spiritual writer Margaret Mary was at last free to do what God had asked of her. She spent the next four years left in her life doing all she could to spread the devotion.

Why is this devotion so important?

Since the time of Fr Colombiere, who has now been canonised, the Jesuits have been given a special role in promoting the devotion to the sacred heart. Margaret Mary herself predicted this. It fits so well with Ignatian spirituality. In 1981 Fr Pedro Arrupe, who had been General of the society for 20 years, made a personal confession to his confreres:

> Since my novitiate, I have always been convinced that what we call 'Devotion to the Sacred Heart' is a symbolic expression of the very basis of the Ignatian spirit, and an extraordinarily effective means of attaining all that we desire – as much for gaining personal perfection as for apostolic success. I still have this conviction.

In 1982 Pope John Paul II on the occasion of the beatification of Claude de la Colombiere wrote a letter to Fr Kolvenback SJ, the General of the Order at that time, in which he said:

> In the Heart of Christ, man's heart learns to know the genuine and unique meaning of his life and of his destiny, to understand the value of an authentically Christian life, to keep himself from certain perversions of the human heart, and to unite the filial love for God and the love of neighbour.

In other words devotion to the heart of Jesus is central to what we are about as Christians. It is an authentically gospel way of life and ought to be lived by all.

Pope Benedict XVI, in a letter written to Fr Kolvenbach on the 50th anniversary of Pope Pius XII's encyclical on the heart of Jesus, states:

> It is only possible to be Christian by fixing our gaze on the Cross of our Redeemer, 'on him whom they have pierced' (Jn 19: 37; cf. Zc 12: 10). God's love is found in the gift Christ made of his life for us on the Cross, the deepest expression of God's love, it is above all by looking at his suffering and his death that we can see God's infinite love for us more and more clearly.

Pope Benedict went on to say that the primary content of the devotion to the heart of Jesus is the mystery of God's immense, unconditional love for us made visible in Christ. He notes that, in fact, this is the content of all true spirituality. Consequently, it is "important to stress that the basis of this devotion is as old as Christianity itself". The heart of what it is to be Christian means that we gaze upon the crucified Christ pierced with a lance for our sake and we make a heartfelt response of love. It is a personal encounter with Christ, the incarnate Son of God, and a wholehearted response to his love. Like Thomas, the apostle, when we encounter the wounds of the crucified and risen Christ we must fall to our knees and worship, "My Lord and my God!" (Jn20:28).

Pope Benedict observes that the experience of love, brought by dwelling upon the pierced side of the Redeemer, protects us from the risk of withdrawing into ourselves and makes us readier to live for others. "By this we know love, that he laid down his life for us; and we ought to lay down our lives for the brethren" (I John 3: 16).

The Significance of the Heart of Jesus

God's love was made visible in the humanity of Jesus, and manifest most fully when he suffered and died for us. The fire of love in the heart of Jesus is unquenchable. "Love is a fire of the heart of God that no floods can quench and no floods drown" (Song 8:6). When we gaze upon Jesus' side opened on the Cross we see the fire of his love for us and our hearts are won over. His heart opened up on the Cross for us conquers our hearts with love and persuades us to yield fully to him. The fire of love in his heart ignites a fire in us, and we burn with love for him, full of gratitude and praise for his immense goodness and mercy.

When his love begins to burn in our hearts we find ourselves full of love for others. His sacrificial love evokes in us the desire to give all for the sake of others. We begin to see the world through the eyes of his heart of love; we want to be crucified with him so that selfishness can be broken in us and we can love as he has loved. As we are drawn more into the fire of love in his heart on the Cross we also feel with him for the lost of this world. We share is his grief as his heart is wrenched for those who are harassed and dejected like sheep without a shepherd. We experience his thirst for souls and have a new urgency to proclaim the Good News of Jesus for the salvation of all men and women.

ALPHONSUS LIGUORI

Chronology

1696 - born in Naples

1722 - experiences conversion

1726 - ordained priest

1732 - leaves Naples to start new congregation

1749 - papal approval of the congregation

1762 - appointed bishop of Agatha of the Goths

1779 - tricked into signing a false rule

1787 - dies on 1 August at Pagani.

Quotes

Acquire the habit of speaking to God
as if you were alone with him,
intimately, with confidence and love,
as to the dearest and most loving friend.

My redeemer, draw me completely to
your love for the sake of the love which
made you die for me on the cross. I love
you, my Jesus, I love you with my whole
soul. This is my goal in life: to love you
always, my highest good.
The past is no longer yours;
the future is not yet in your power.
You have only the present
wherein to do good.

He who trusts in himself is lost.

He who trusts in God can do all things.

ALPHONSUS LIGUORI

Born in 1696 in Naples, Alphonsus was the eldest of eight children. His devout mother ran the household with a discipline akin to a religious novitiate, while his father, a Navy captain, harboured high ambitions for his first born son.[154] As a child Alphonsus learnt Italian, Latin, Greek, French, science, maths, art, architecture, music and philosophy. Precocious and brilliant, by age 17, four years before the legal age, he had passed his doctoral examination in law with honours. Then as a young man in eight years of legal practice he never lost a case. Rich, successful and popular, he had the world at his feet. Deeply spiritual in temperament he would spend an hour before the Blessed Sacrament every day. At the age of 26, while on a retreat conducted by the Vincentians, he experienced a deep encounter with the Lord; deciding to resist his father's attempts to get him married, he made a private vow of celibacy.

The Call

Then a crisis hit this successful young man's life. Handling a simple case over an estate claim which involved large sums of money, he overlooked a clause in fine print in a document which decided the case in favour of his opponent. Alphonsus, the perfectionist, was humiliated. He cried out, "Ah, world, I know you now!" Returning home he locked himself in his room for three days. He begged the Lord to show him what he was to do with his life. The answer came in a gentle, appealing voice in his soul, "Give yourself to me!" Alphonsus ended his legal career and, regardless of his father's violent objections, decided to enter the priesthood. He became a diocesan seminarian.

Even as a seminarian Alphonsus became a member of the Apostolic Missions, a group of priests who were dedicated to popular mission preaching. Their spiritual mentor was Francis de Sales whose spirituality inspired them. They promoted the Forty Hours devotion before the exposed Blessed Sacrament and every year had an Ignatian retreat under the *Spiritual Exercises*. Their highly organised evangelistic programs involved preaching, catechesis, confessions, and Eucharistic adoration. When he was ordained a priest, Alphonsus' simple, direct, evangelistic style became popular, and people were attracted to his confessional, because unlike the customary rigorist style of the day, he was gentle and merciful in approach. He and his companions reached out to the inner city poor, and soon a movement known as the "Evening chapel" developed as the groups of poor lay people from all over the city met together to pray and learn about their faith.

The Mission

Exhausted from preaching many missions, Alphonsus and his friends were taking a well-earned holiday. Travelling by sea they were caught in a storm near the Amalfi Coast and decided to remain at a place just outside the town of Scala for their vacation. No sooner had they arrived than they were inundated with visits from local shepherds who were starving for the gospel. Alphonsus was moved by these poor country folk who were ignorant of the fundamentals of their faith, without any spiritual care and so hungry for the word of God and the sacraments. It deeply troubled him that within a few days' journey of Naples these people, spiritually abandoned and neglected, were without help. He was well aware that in Naples there was a surfeit of priests, since many were ordained as a way for the family property to escape taxation. In the city there was an average of one priest to every 100 citizens, and many of them lived with their families. Alphonsus and his friends abandoned the idea of a holiday and spent their time preaching missions, instructing the people in the faith, hearing confessions, celebrating Mass and leading the people in adoration of Jesus in the Blessed Sacrament and praying the rosary.

The Vision

In 1731 while Alphonsus was giving a retreat in a convent in Scala, Sister Maria Celeste revealed to him she had a vision of a new congregation devoted to the work of the Redeemer. Even though others considered her vision to be delusory, Alphonsus was convinced it was true. Supported by his spiritual director he began the new foundation in a guesthouse to the Convent in Scala until he could find other accommodation. Beginning with three priests and the promise of four others to come he made a start. It was a rocky beginning. After six months of dispute over vision, the Rule, and leadership, all three deserted him. Left alone he was tempted to despair. Yet it wasn't long before others caught the vision and the little congregation began to expand and flourish. They spent themselves generously in preaching missions to the small towns and villages, providing catechesis, the sacraments, and teaching them to pray.

In addition to leading the congregation and conducting missions Alphonsus was a prolific writer of books and pastoral pamphlets. One of the Church's most prominent moral theologians, and recognised now as a doctor of the Church, his books on morality steered a middle path through the extremes of rigorism and laxism, emphasising the importance of an informed conscience so that people could make good and right moral decisions, as a response to the love of God. Nine editions of his great work *Moral Theology* were published in his lifetime. But amongst the other 110 titles he regarded his devotional masterpiece, *The Practice of the Love of Jesus Christ*, published in 1768, the most useful of all his writings.

Surprisingly Alphonsus had a life-long struggle with scruples, an obsessive compulsive disorder which generates irrational thoughts and feelings of guilt so that even small misdemeanours can seem displeasing to God. His practical solution to the problem was to pledge absolute obedience to his spiritual director, who could relieve him of anxiety whenever he thought he had lost God's favour. Amazingly, even though the root of this disorder is in a flawed notion of God as a hard taskmaster, Alphonsus was used by God to bring a most inspiring and liberating message of the love of God in all his spiritual writings. It is a remarkable testimony of the victory of God's love in a profoundly broken human vessel.

Later Life

By 1761, the 65-year-old priest was in semi-retirement at the congregation's monastery in Pagani, partially deaf, blind, and asthmatic, and suffering from a wounded leg which caused him to limp. Yet retirement was not in God's plan for him! In 1762 Pope Clement XIII appointed him Bishop of St Agatha of the Goths, a diocese near Naples. Alphonsus begged the Pope to change his mind, without success. For 13 years he was a bishop of the poor. He wore a glass ring and a simple iron cross. His table was frugal, no matter who was attending. He sought to establish a missionary diocese, and was renowned for his love of the poor. Finally at the age of 80 years the Pope accepted his resignation. He lived another 12 years suffering from a disease that caused such curvature in his neck that his chin pressed against his chest, causing a deep open wound.

Unfortunately the physical suffering Alphonsus was called to endure was nothing in comparison to what he experienced from the betrayal of his own brethren. Of the eight monasteries of the congregation, four were in the Papal States and four under the kingdom of Naples. The congregation had already received Papal approval in 1749, but it had yet to receive the approval of the King of Naples which was necessary for its continued existence. Alphonsus sent two trusted advisers to the court of Naples to obtain the approval. But on the insistence of the King, the Rule became severely compromised. These brothers tricked Alphonsus, who was almost blind, into signing this new Rule without being aware of its contents. When he learnt what he had done he wept in anguish: "I have been betrayed!"

Then the leaders of the houses in the Papal States decided to seek Papal endorsement for those houses holding to the original Rule as authentic. Consequently, Pius VI signed a decree that effectively dismissed the members of the houses in Naples from the congregation! On 1 August 1787 Alphonsus died, no longer a member of the congregation he had founded! Thankfully he died peacefully, in complete surrender to the Lord, and in following years the division in the congregation was rectified.

A Symphony of Love

Alphonsus was largely indebted to Francis de Sales and Ignatius Loyola for his spiritual theology. Although his writings are interspersed with quotations from a whole range of spiritual sources, such as Bernard of Clairvaux, Augustine of Hippo, Thomas Aquinas, Teresa of Avila, John of the Cross, and many more. His central focus is on the love of God revealed to us in Jesus crucified and the way we are to best obtain this love and live accordingly. He was overwhelmed by the excessive love that God has for us and how much God desires our generous love for him in return. Because we have been loved so lavishly, the only response worthy of this gift is to love him unconditionally with our whole lives.[155] Alphonsus understood grace in the same way as Francis de Sales.

God has taken the initiative and seeks to win us by his love. His love for us is unconditional, and, because it is love, it seeks union with the beloved. He seeks to captivate us with his love. He has firstly given us the beauty of his creation, and surrounded us with countless gifts. All creation's beauty speaks of God's immense love for us. It awakens in us gratitude and a desire to praise him, and return his love with all our hearts.

Secondly, when we had sinned and separated ourselves from him, he could not bear to be without us. So in his great love he chose to become one of us in order to redeem us. Love seeks union. His unconditional love for us led him to take on our frail human flesh in such a way that our stubborn wills would melt, and softened by his appeal, we would be drawn to respond. Christmas day for Alphonsus was a "day of fire", as we are stirred in our hearts by this defenceless child lying in swaddling clothes, God with us, choosing to be born in a stable not fit for human beings, and being laid in a manger, a feeding trough for animals. The whole purpose is to win us back to him. What could be less threatening, and more appealing, than a child in a manger? He came with none of the trappings of worldly power and grandeur that we usually associate with royalty, but in poverty and humility, to break open our hearts in love for him.

The third movement in this symphony of love is the excessive love for us which took Jesus to the Cross for our sake. He was put to death as a criminal. During his life on earth he longed with all his heart to be able to give himself completely for us. The Cross was his "hour"; the appointed time to show "how perfect his love was" (Jn.13:1). During his preaching he had said, "I have come to bring fire to the earth, and how I wish it were blazing already" (Lk 12:49). He was speaking of the fire of love for us already burning in his heart, which he would demonstrate outwardly in his passion. He suffered so that he could win us to himself. Our hard and obstinate hearts melt and become enflamed with love for him when we consider his passion, the proof of his love for us. We are won by love. Alphonsus believed that for Christ to redeem us one single perfect act of obedience would have been enough to overturn the disobedience of the human race. While the extreme suffering of the passion was not necessary it was his way of showing the excess of his love for us. "What a drop of his blood would have done he chose to do with a stream". This excessive love was his way of winning us back to him. Quoting Francis de Sales he says, "With what love would we not be set on fire at the sight of those flames which burn in the breast of the Redeemer. What a wonderful experience it would be for us to burn with the very fire that consumes our God, and what a joy to be united to God with the chains of love".

The incarnation broke down the natural barrier between us and God. The Cross broke down the barrier caused by sin. Yet God's love which seeks union was still not satisfied. He wanted to find a way of union with us here on earth that surpasses all other ways. The fourth great act of love was the master stroke, designed to achieve this end. He emptied himself even further, giving himself to us as food in the Eucharist. At the Last Supper he said "I have longed to eat this Passover with you" (Lk.22:15). The heart of Jesus yearns for union with us, and in the Eucharist this union is effected powerfully for those who are receptive: "He who eats my flesh and drinks my blood abides in me and I in him" (Jn.6:56). This whole story is the initiative of God who has come to us in self-emptying love. It calls forth within us a response of self-emptying love in return. We are to allow him to capture us with his love. Lovers desire that where there were formerly two, there now be one. We allow the bridegroom to take hold of the bride. The whole Christ is given to us in Holy Communion. The divine fire that is in the human heart of Christ sets our hearts burning with love for him; once this fire is alight within us nothing less than complete union will satisfy.

Obtaining the Love of God

In his writings Alphonsus guided his readers towards welcoming the love of God. Again and again he returns to certain conditions and practices that provide the way forward towards responding to his love and coming into union with him.[156]

a) Detachment of heart

He says, "Take the earth from your heart so it may be filled with the love of God". When love enters the heart, other things no longer have the same value. As Francis de Sales says, "All the furniture is thrown out the window when the house is on fire". Love is a fire that burns deeply within us and for love we will be prepared to give up all we have and count nothing of the cost (Song 8:7). God is a jealous lover. He cannot bear us to have a divided heart. We must have undivided love for him. As Paul says "I believe nothing can happen that will outweigh the supreme advantage of knowing Christ Jesus, my Lord. I consider everything else as so much rubbish if only I can have Christ and be given a place in him" (Phil 3:8-9). We need to make our souls a "garden enclosed" and keep the gate closed against all other loves (Song 4:12).

b) Contemplation

He follows Ignatius in the way of meditative prayer which leads to contemplation, "looking long" at Jesus. He urges that we create a space of solitude in the heart to hear the voice of God. Our love for God will only be kept burning by regular times set aside to be alone with him, our best friend. The devil's main temptation is to convince us to let go of prayer. We must constantly stoke the fire of desire for God. The more we desire the Lord the more he will pour his favours upon us.

c) Meditation on the Passion

The flaming love in the heart of Jesus on the cross sets fire to our hearts. He quotes Bonaventure, "There is nothing that has such a universal influence on our spiritual life as meditation on the passion of Christ". Francis of Assisi, who was not given to reading books, when questioned about this replied, "My book is Jesus crucified". Francis is reputed to have lost his sight due to so much weeping as he meditated on the sufferings of Jesus. Every time he heard a bleating of a lamb it would remind him of the sacrifice of the blood shed by the innocent Lamb of God. Paul, when preaching to the Corinthians claimed to know no philosophy or have any great oratorical skills. He claimed only to know Christ, and him crucified (1Cor2:2). Meditating on the passion we are overwhelmed by the love of God and compelled with love for him and for others (2Cor 5:14). As we meditate on the passion of Jesus we are touched by the madness of his love for us. He suffered for us so we would know how great his love is for us and that God would rather be loved than feared. His perfect love drives out all fear. (1Jn 4:18). As we gaze upon Jesus crucified we discover his heart of love for all, and are inspired to follow him in giving up our lives for others (1John 3:16).

d) Eucharist

Alphonsus quotes John Chrysostom, "Eucharist is a burning fuel that starts up a fire within us, so that we come away from the table with the strength of lions, and breathing fire that fills the demons with terror". It says in scripture that "God is a consuming fire" (Deut 4:24); this is the fire of his love; because "God is love" (1Jn 4:8). He follows Francis de Sales in extoling the Eucharist as the tender and loving action of our Saviour, since he "reduces himself to nothing, so to speak, and becomes food" that he may penetrate the depth of our hearts and be united with us forever. In Eucharist he shows how perfect his love is, and urges us to come into union with him (Jn 13:1). He comes that we may abide in him and he in us (Jn 6:56). There is no time in our earthly journey when we can have more intimacy with Jesus than when we receive him in Holy Communion; this should always be a time of closeness and attentiveness to his presence and his voice within us.

e) Conformity of our will with God's will

The real test of our love for God is not so much by taking on extra penances to prove our love, but by willingly accepting the difficulties, trials and calamities of life which come to us unexpectedly, accepting them as the will of God for us. When sickness, suffering, and other adversities which we are unable to change come upon us, we are being given an opportunity to grow in the love of God by a share in the suffering of Christ. Contrary to the popular asceticism of his time, Alphonsus would say that surrendering to the will of God in times of adversity is better than a 1,000 fasts or scourgings. He quotes John of Avila, "One 'blessed be God' in time of affliction is worth 1,000 'Praise Gods' in a time of prosperity". We are to find rest in the arms of God at all times, both in prosperity and adversity.

f) Prayer of Petition

Alphonsus wants us to acknowledge our poverty before God. We have nothing, and so must ask him confidently for everything, "Ask and it shall be given" (Luke11:9). Begging of the Lord is a sign of our love for him; he wants to lavish his love upon us when we ask him. We have absolute need of God's help to overcome temptations; we cannot survive in the journey without his help, which he readily gives when we ask.

Alphonsus wrote a little pamphlet on the necessity of the prayer of petition.[157] In the preface he says that there is nothing more important for preachers and spiritual directors to know than the necessity of petitionary prayer. In God's ordinary providence he does not give the help of grace unless we ask him. God who created us without our cooperation will not save us without our cooperation. The Lord permits temptations so that we would cry out to him for help and realise our incapacity to save ourselves. We need to ask the Lord with humility and with confidence; God resists the proud and listens to the cry of the poor (Ps 33:18-90). And we must persevere. He wants us to "do violence to him" with our prayers. Like the widow pleading with the unjust judge who pestered him persistently (Lk 18:1-8), or like the importunate neighbour who would not give up knocking on the door of his neighbour for the bread he needed (Lk 11:5-8), we too must persist in prayer until the Lord answers.

When the Lord delays to answer our prayers, Alphonsus says not to be discouraged. He just wants to prove our confidence in him, or increase our longing for the gift desired. Otherwise we may be like a spoilt child who obtains everything immediately upon asking and does not appreciate the gift. By delaying to give to us the Lord is helping us to grow in love of him. The main thing is not to give up asking with confidence and perseverance.

Missions

Alphonsus' missionary work needs to be understood in the context from which it originated. The main outlines of Neapolitan missions were well in place before he began his priestly ministry and well before his congregation of preachers was launched. Nevertheless, Alphonsus was aware of the inadequacies of the mission style that he had inherited and he began to innovate. He understood that a mission to a town or village conducted by his brothers was as an opportunity for the people to encounter Christ in a new way and to come to a new level of personal conversion. Each mission was a continuation of the redeeming action of Jesus in the world today. It was not only aimed at inveterate sinners, but to everyone, no matter what state of their soul. Remembering that, in eighteenth century Italy, most people were at least nominal Catholics the missions had a strong tone of re-evangelisation or what we would call a "new evangelisation". They were intended to wake people up from their lethargic and lukewarm faith and bring the new fire of conversion to Christ. The simple preaching of the word of God; the inspiring teachings on doctrinal and moral issues relevant to the lives of people; the challenge to change their way of life to conform more to the will of God; the re-acquaintance with the sacraments; the introduction to a personal life of prayer; all of this was aimed towards allowing the redeeming and sanctifying love of God to bring fire to hearts again.

The ministry of the confessional was central to the success of the missions. Alphonsus instructed his priests to be merciful and patient in the confessional, not to be harsh, demanding and threatening like many of their contemporary priests. They were never to discourage penitents, but to encourage them to higher things. Each mission would offer seven hours of confessional ministry daily, shared by a number of priests. If a priest became tired he was not to stay in the confessional, but to walk around outside for a while until he was in a better mood. Alphonsus' own experience in the confessional was remarkably patient, and cost him much due to his natural impetuous temperament. Inclined to become irritable he had to fight himself. He described the confessional as a file which silently but painfully smooths the irritability of one's character. Contrary to the practice of the day, he encouraged his priests never to dismiss a penitent without granting absolution, unless this was canonically impossible. Alphonsus did not only see this sacrament as a balm for those in serious sin, but also as an opportunity of grace for those seeking to grow in holiness.

Evangelical Style

When preaching a mission Alphonsus required that the brothers keep to simple food without any delicacies or treats. Anything that could be regarded as the food of the nobility would be banned. They were to wear their habit without any adornments, so that they keep in touch with the poor. The missioners were not to stand on rank, but greet people kindly and respectfully. Poor country folk were not accustomed to being saluted by someone of a higher social rank, but Alphonsus wanted to win them by courtesy and respect for their inherent dignity as persons. He told his priests that even if they were not saints at home in the monastery, they needed to be genuinely men of patience, kindness and charity when on mission.

The mission team was usually about a dozen or so, including some lay brothers and seminarians. Sometimes it comprised more, any number up to about 20 members. When they arrived in the village on foot the church bells would ring and people would gather in the town square. Occasionally the parish priest refused to welcome them, but they always came under the auspices of the bishop. The parish would usually accommodate them and where possible they maintained their common life of prayer, singing the Office and daily hour before the Blessed Sacrament throughout the time of the mission. During the early days of the mission the priests and brothers would move around the village drawing attention to the mission and inviting people to come. They would preach short exhortations in the market square or in more isolated places. At night they would go around with a large crucifix and lighted torches, chanting the Litany of Our Lady, stopping outside taverns or wherever people were likely to gather.

The primary event of the mission was the daily evening sermon in the church when most of the people would gather. It would last about an hour and a half. This was followed by the recitation of the rosary and an instruction on some doctrinal matter. In the mornings there was a meditation with the people and further instruction. Alphonsus put great emphasis upon the catechetical element, since the people were so often ignorant of the fundamentals of the faith. He regarded the catechesis to be as important as the preaching if not more so. It had to be practical and apply directly to people's lives, helping people to conduct their daily life well in imitation of Jesus.

The whole mission was meant to be a complete work of spiritual renewal. Alphonsus emphasised the "devout life", taken from Francis de Sales. By this he meant taking people through "exercises" which inflamed their hearts with love towards Jesus crucified. The main feature of this was meditative prayer. The people were instructed on how to reflect upon the mysteries of Christ in the manner of Ignatius, as given by Francis de Sales. Then they were led through a meditation by one of the missioners. The people were also instructed on how to make a visit to the Blessed Sacrament. He devoted special times for Eucharistic adoration, encouraging people to use his little book on how to make visits to the Lord. To keep the spiritual life going after the missioners left they established sodalities for different groupings of people so they would continue to support one another in a new life with the Lord.

Preachers of the Redemption

The motto of the new congregation, which we now call the "Redemptorists", was "With the Lord there is mercy and fullness of redemption" (Psalm 130:7). Alphonsus' emphasis was on the "fullness of redemption". From the initial vision of Sr Marie

Celeste they were to be "preachers of the redemption". Similar to St Paul, who reminded the Corinthians, "When I came among you the only knowledge I claimed to have was about Jesus, and only about him as the crucified Christ" (1Cor 2:2), they simply preached the redemption won for us in Jesus Christ. This was the heart of their preaching endeavour and the reason for its phenomenal success.

In Naples of the 18th century sacred eloquence had become florid in style, highly ornate, and beyond the reach of ordinary people. It was an art of speaking somewhat akin to the baroque architectural style of the time; so elaborate that it left people cold. The sermon was no longer an explanation of scripture or a proclamation of Christ. It was an art form in its own right. The Lenten preachings in large churches were prize appointments and attracted huge crowds who attended for the spectacle but went away untouched in their hearts. The great "preachers" of the day were stylised prima donnas who gave forth with vapid rhetoric which was largely meaningless to the common person and with no application to daily life. Alphonsus adamantly opposed this manner of preaching and forbad his priests to get involved in it. Of this type of preaching he says:

> What a tragedy it is to see so many ordinary people going to these sermons in order to learn what they should do to save their souls, and after listening to the preacher for more than and an hour and a half, they find they have learnt nothing. They return home as empty as they arrived and disgusted with themselves for wasting all that time in listening to a sermon which they did not understand.[158]

Preaching Love, not Fear

Alphonsus' style was simple, clear, direct and eminently practical. He spoke the language people understood, using phrases and expressions in their own dialect. He said, "One must lose oneself in the spirit of the people when preaching to them, otherwise, you get as far as their ears, but you do not touch their hearts". There were no flourishes of rhetoric or pompous language or dramatic modulations. Rather there was conviction of the heart and proclamation of the truth of our redemption in Christ. His style was personal, more like a conversation than a sermon. He drew the listener by his authentically holy life and his witness of love.

Before he rose to preach he would spend a long time in prayer, no doubt praying that the Lord would use his words and the Spirit would open the hearts of the listeners. Without the anointing of the Holy Spirit a preacher is but a futile orator. His words were never abusive or condemning; rather he won people by gentleness, and the persuasion which truth itself brings when proclaimed in the Spirit. He called this "apostolic" preaching, because it was centred in Jesus crucified, relying on the power of the Holy Spirit, rising out of prayer, proclaimed with personal conviction, and meeting people in their own life-situation, calling them to conversion, and having a lasting impact on their lives.

The sermons in the missions of the day usually focused on death, judgment, hell and heaven. The emphasis was on putting the fear of hell into people to change their behaviour. Alphonsus, while keeping these topics in his repertoire, moved away from the "terror" tradition. He insisted on every mission having topics on the love of God, the passion of Jesus Christ, prayer and Our Lady. He conceded that sermons on judgment and hell can stir people. But he noted that

> Conversions merely from terror do not last – these motives are soon forgotten. But whoever is converted through consideration of the love of Jesus Christ, their conversion is more genuine and lasting. Fear will not achieve what love can achieve. Sometimes a

sermon which causes fear can be dismissed with a shrug of the shoulder but one spark of the love of God is sufficient to burn up everything else.[159]

For Alphonsus the test for a genuine missionary preacher was to leave his congregation inflamed with the love of God after every sermon. Sadly this perspective was lost later in the Redemptorist congregation when the motive of fear of judgment and hell became prominent in popular preachers.

The central focus of Alphonsus' preaching was the love of God revealed in the passion of Christ. He urged his priests to always preach love for Jesus crucified. As a bishop he commissioned a large realistic life-size painting of the crucifixion. He wanted to give visual impact to the words he preached. If he was preaching today he would be using audio-visuals to gain the same effect. At the end of the mission he would have the painting brought through the church for veneration of the people and then brought to the pulpit as one of the priests preached a fervent message on the love of Jesus Christ in his passion. It was well known among the missioners that if some sinner had resisted the grace of the mission during the early days of preaching he was sure to repent after the crucifix ceremony.

THERESE OF LISIEUX

Chronology

1873 - born in Alencon, France

1882 - Pauline joins Carmel

1884 - first communion grace

1886 - Christmas grace; a new conversion

1895 - consecration to Merciful Love of God

1896 - completed Manuscript A and B

1897 - completed Manuscript C

       Therese dies on 30th September in Lisieux

Quotes

Sanctity does not consist in this or that practice; it consists in a disposition of heart which makes us humble and little in the arms of God, conscious of our weakness, and confident to the point of audacity in the goodness of our Father

For me, prayer is a surge of the heart; it is a simple look turned toward heaven, it is a cry of recognition and of love, embracing both trial and joy. Miss no single opportunity of making some small sacrifice, here by a smiling look, there by a kindly word; always doing the smallest right and doing it all for love.

Even if I had all the crimes possible on my conscience I am sure I would lose none of my confidence. I would simply throw myself into my Saviour's arms, for I know how much he loves the prodigal child ... I know that in a twinkling of an eye all those thousands of sins would be consumed as a drop of water cast into a burning fire.

THERESE OF LISIEUX

Therese was born into a close-knit family on 2 January 1873 at Alencon, in Normandy. At the age of four Therese lost her mother who died of breast cancer. She chose Pauline, her favourite sister to be her second mother. When she was only nine years old she lost Pauline who had decided to enter the Carmelite convent at Lisieux, Therese was so distressed at this loss that she fell seriously ill with a kind of nervous breakdown and delirium. Her cure came miraculously through a smile of the Blessed Virgin which she saw on a statue in her room. Marie, the eldest child, now became Therese's confidante and spiritual guide. We get a picture of the extraordinary love that the Lord was awakening in Therese's soul as we read her account of her experience of first Holy Communion at the age of eleven.

> Ah! How sweet was that first kiss of Jesus! It was a kiss of love; I felt that I was loved, and I said: 'I love you, and I give myself to you forever!' There were no demands made, no struggles, no sacrifices; for a long time now Jesus and poor little Therese looked at and understood each other. That day, it was no longer simply a look, it was a fusion; they were no longer two, Therese had vanished as a drop of water is lost in the immensity of the ocean. Jesus alone remained; He was the Master, the King.[160]

The Christmas Grace

Therese was to suffer a further blow when two years later Marie also entered the convent at Lisieux. With all the emotional losses she had undergone she had become overly sensitive to how others perceived her and inclined to become upset at trivial things. She was aware of this problem but was powerless to overcome it. One disapproving look from a significant other would reduce her to tears. Then at the age of fourteen the Lord came to her aid. She experienced what she later called her "Christmas grace". The family had a custom of leaving presents in her shoes left in the chimney corner. Her "papa" who doted on his "little queen" had always loved to see the delight in her eyes as she drew out her present from the magic shoes. However, this Christmas night in 1886 when the family arrived home from midnight Mass her father was tired and seeing her shoes by the fireplace, groaned, "Well, fortunately, this will be the last year!" Overhearing these words as she was going up the stairs Therese was hurt deeply, feeling sorry for herself, and wanted to cry. But at that moment she experienced a grace from God for which she was forever grateful. Instead of dissolving into a blubbering mess and succumbing to the offended feelings of self-pity, she had the strength to shrug it off and joyfully open her presents.

She said, "The work I had been unable to do in ten years was done by Jesus in one instant".[161] She felt like the apostles who had been fishing all night and caught nothing: "More merciful to me than he was to his disciples, Jesus took the net himself, cast it, and drew it in filled with fish. He made me a fisher of souls. I experienced a great desire to work for the conversion of sinners, a desire I hadn't felt so intensely before". A change was happening in her soul, which was sheer grace from God. She no longer was trapped in her self-centred sensitivity. "I felt charity enter into my soul, and the need to forget myself and to please others; since then I've been happy!" She relates how soon after this experience she was looking at a picture of Jesus on the Cross. She was drawn to be at the foot of the Cross and rather than let his blood fall to the ground she wanted to pour it out upon souls. "The cry of Jesus on the Cross sounded continually in my heart: 'I thirst!' These words ignited within me an unknown and very living fire. I wanted to give my Beloved to drink and I felt myself consumed with a thirst for souls".[162]

Then in 1887 she had a striking opportunity to put into practice this new-found love for sinners. She heard about an infamous criminal, named Henri Pranzini who had been condemned to death and was unrepentant for his crimes. She prayed unremittingly for his soul, that the merciful Lord would pardon his sins. She absolutely trusted that the Lord in all mercy would answer her prayers; yet she asked the Lord for a sign. After the execution she was able to get her hands on a newspaper and was delighted to read that even though Pranzini had not gone to confession, when on the scaffold before his beheading he unexpectedly seized hold of the crucifix that the priest-chaplain was holding out to him and kissed the holy wounds of Jesus three times. That was the "sign" she had requested. She was jubilant. This intercessory triumph was a defining moment for her life.

Six months after her "Christmas grace" Therese was convinced she was meant to enter Carmel and she revealed her intentions to her father, who accepted her wishes. But it was a matter of convincing the bishop to allow her to enter at fifteen years old, which was even in those days far younger than was usually acceptable. Remarkably she gained permission and joined her two sisters in Carmel at Lisieux in 1888. In the following year her father, suffering with mental illness, was hospitalised. He was to die in 1894. Therese's sister Celine who had taken upon herself to nurse their father was now free herself to join Carmel. By that time Therese herself only had less than three years before she died on 30 September 1897.

The Story of a Soul

Therese's spirituality became best known through the *Story of a Soul,* which was really three different manuscripts put together for publication after her death. Manuscript A was written during 1895. In the previous year, Pauline, now Mother Agnes had become the Prioress of the convent and she asked Therese to write her childhood memories. Written in her spare time for her family members the story was presented by Therese as a way of singing the mercies of God she had experienced in her short life. The manuscript took about a year to complete. Done out of obedience, she was totally detached from it, not caring what happened to it. Manuscript B is dated 8 September 1896, about a year and a half before her death. It was requested by and addressed to her sister Marie, whose religious name was Sr Marie of the Sacred Heart. Therese writes to Jesus "since this makes it easier to express my thoughts". Her intimacy with Jesus was such that she was more comfortable opening her heart to him than to any lesser friend, even her blood sister whom she loved. It is only ten pages but is considered the "jewel" of all her writings, since it clearly speaks of Therese's "little way" and also includes her famous account of how she discovered "my vocation is love". Manuscript C is dated June 1897, less than three months from Therese's death. Pauline, who as we have seen was Mother Agnes, had been succeeded as Prioress by Mother Gonzague. Pauline was aware that Therese was dying and the original story of her life was incomplete, not giving enough about Therese's religious life. On the pretext of gaining information for Therese's obituary she convinced Mother Gonzague to order Therese to finish her story. It is mainly about her life in Carmel and especially her suffering and the "night of faith" that accompanied it.

The Little Way

Therese always wanted to be a saint. But when she looked at the physical penances and mortifications that she supposed saints had to perform in order to please God she felt unable to emulate them. Before the demand of rigorous asceticism, the conventional way to sainthood, she felt powerless. Having a great desire for holiness she felt the goal was utterly unattainable. But she did not lose heart: "Instead of becoming discouraged, I said to myself: God cannot inspire unrealisable desires. I can, then, in spite of my littleness, aspire to holiness".[163] Her desire for holiness could not be futile; there must be a way.

She decided to find her own way to holiness, confident that God would provide it. "I want to seek out a means of going to heaven by a little way, a way that is very straight, very short and totally new".[164] Ever creative in the Spirit, Therese remembered elevators, a new invention, which she had seen on her earlier visit to Rome. This became her image for her little way, "I wanted to find an elevator which would raise me to Jesus, for I am too small to climb the rough stairway of perfection".[165]

She then began to search in the Scriptures for a spiritual elevator "that would raise me to Jesus". She had available to her a number of Old Testament texts which Celine had collected and brought in a small book with her to the convent. Here she found the vital text: "Whoever is a little one, let him come to me" (Prov 9:4). This text spoke personally to her that all she had to do was to come to the Lord as a little one. She then searched further to know what this could mean. She came upon, "As one whom a mother caresses, so will I comfort you; you shall be carried at the breasts, and upon the knees they shall caress you" (Is 66:13, 12). Now she knew the answer! The elevator that would raise her to heaven was the very arms of Jesus. "And for this I had no reason to grow up, but rather to remain little and become this more and more". All she had to do was acknowledge her powerlessness, littleness and inability, and to trust fully in Jesus who would lift her up in his loving arms. In a letter to Pauline, who had asked about the little way, Therese replied:

> It is to recognise our nothingness, to expect everything from God as a little child expects everything from its father; it is to be disquieted about nothing, and not to be set on gaining our living... To be little is not attributing to oneself the virtues that one

practices, believing oneself capable of anything, but to recognise that God places this treasure in the hands of his little child to be used when necessary; but it remains always God's treasure. Finally, it is not to become discouraged over one's faults, for children fall often, but they are too little to hurt themselves much.[166]

Knowing our Inner Poverty

Therese tells us not to worry about our imperfections. If we are strong and self-sufficient we don't need God's help. He is attracted to us precisely because of our weakness and dependency upon him. There is no point in trying to make ourselves look great before him; in that case we are saying we don't need him. She says:

> Look at little children. They constantly break things, tear them up, fall, and all the while, in spite of that, they love their parents very much. Well, when I fall in this way, like a child, it makes me realize my nothingness and weakness all the better and I say to myself: 'What would become of me? What would I be able to accomplish if I were to rely on my own powers alone?' God loves to show his strength through our weakness. We must humbly take our place among the imperfect, and know our littleness, being in need of God's help at every instant. When he sees we are truly convinced of our nothingness he will extend his hand to help us.

Therese understood how hard it is to take this little way. We are prone to try and manage without the Lord. In today's world we especially want to be independent and self-sufficient and find it difficult to be as a child, even though Jesus said, "Unless you change and become like a little child you shall not enter the Kingdom of God" (Matthew 18:3). We need to accept that we own nothing; everything we have that is good comes as a gift from God. It is not easy for us to accept our powerlessness, poverty, misery and dependence. We are pressured in the world to be in total control of our lives. The way to heaven is the exact opposite; we give over the control to the Lord. This way of Therese involves a total surrender to the Lord who is All for us.

At the end of her life one of the sisters caring for her said, "You must have struggled very much to reach your degree of perfection". She replied, "It is not that at all. Sanctity does not consist in this or that practice. It consists in a disposition of heart which make us humble and little in God's arms, conscious of our weakness and confident even to audacity in the goodness of our Father".[167]

To attain holiness, Therese taught the importance of doing good works. But these alone do not establish the progress. Rather they are a statement of our good will and right disposition. She uses a graphic image to make the point:

> Be like a little child. Practice all the virtues and so always lift up your little foot to mount the stairway of holiness. But do not imagine that you will be able to ascend over the first step. No. The good Lord does not demand more from you than good will. From the top of the stairs he looks at you with love. Very soon, won over by your useless efforts, he will come down and take you in his arms. He will carry you up. But if you stop lifting your little foot, he will leave you a long time on the ground.

Confidence in the Mercy of God

Therese's little way means never to become discouraged with our faults and failings. When we sin it is simply a matter of repenting and throwing ourselves confidently on the mercy of God. She says that discouragement springs from self-love, from a refusal to acknowledge our true condition of soul. It is a rebellion against our littleness. She warns, "To brood gloomily over our own imperfection paralyses the soul".[168] We do more harm to ourselves through discouragement after we have fallen than by the fall itself. When we have fallen we must with true sorrow abandon ourselves into the merciful arms of Jesus. "He measures his gifts according to the measure of confidence he finds in us." She insists that what offends Jesus more than our faults and failings is our lack of confidence in his mercy. This is what wounds his heart most. We act as if his heart is not big enough to contain and embrace our miserable sins.

Therese uses some quaint images to express this truth. She encourages us, "it is a matter of taking hold of Jesus by his heart".[169] She asks us to imagine a little child who has just annoyed his mother by flying into a temper or by disobeying her. If he hides in a corner feeling sorry for himself, sulking and fearful of punishment, he may be there in misery for a long time. But if he comes to her, holding out his arms, smiling and saying, "Kiss me, Mama, I will not do it again", what mother would not take him into her arms, hold him to her heart, and kiss him tenderly? This is what Jesus is like. Though the mother knows the little one will probably misbehave again at the first opportunity, that means nothing if the child appeals to her heart.

Therese's sister Marie said she asked Therese whether God was displeased with her because of her imperfections. Therese answered by saying that God's love for us blinds him from seeing our sins. And he is ignorant of mathematics; he cannot count. We count others' faults against them, but he does not. We must take him by his heart, this is his weak spot. She continued:

> Look at it this way. If the greatest sinner on earth repented of all his offences at the last moment and died in an act of love, God would not stop to weigh up the numerous graces which the unfortunate man had wasted and the crimes he had been guilty of; he counts only that last prayer and receives him into the arms of his mercy without delay.[170]

Consecration to God's Merciful Love

In Therese's time Jansenism still had a hold to some degree on religious life. Her sisters were used to making a consecration to the justice of God, as if this was the highest attribute in God. They would offer themselves as victims to God's justice 'in order to turn away the punishments reserved to sinners, drawing them upon themselves".[171] This aspiration did not attract Therese at all! Instead she was inspired to offer herself as a "victim" to God's merciful love. While she knew the importance of God's justice, it was his mercy which she found to be his paramount quality. "How much more does your merciful love desire to set souls on fire since your mercy reaches to the heavens. O my Jesus, let me be this happy victim; consume your holocaust with the fire of your divine love!"[172]

The primary image of the Jansenist God was that of a tyrant exacting strict justice. He was a demanding, oppressive God, holding people in fear of eternal punishment if they did not keep his commandments perfectly. There was a lack of genuine love for God. People were trying to avoid sin and keep the commandments not out of love for God but out of fear of punishment. In stark contrast to this Therese viewed all the qualities of God through the lens of his mercy. The name she gave to God was Merciful Love. Her letters to the young missionary priest, Maurice Belliere, are a moving example of her appreciation of the mercy of God.[173] Maurice was constantly dogged by the shame and guilt of a sinful past and found it difficult to know God's mercy for him. She draws his attention to Mary Magdalene who was so filled with gratitude for God's mercy to her that she boldly entered a Pharisee's house and before hostile eyes threw herself at his feet with tears of thanksgiving. She was not looking at herself, no longer burdened by the sins of her past, not relying upon her own credit which was worthless, but simply looked at Jesus and saw his merciful love towards her. This brought her into intimacy with him. Therese urged Maurice to do the same.

Therese tirelessly insisted that we can never have too much confidence in the mercy and power of the Lord to lift us up, no matter what our situation is before him. The main thing is to be utterly confident in his mercy. This is the difference between Peter and Judas. Both sinned grievously. But Judas despaired, losing all trust in the mercy of God which was offered to him. Peter wept bitterly for his sin, but did not despair. Looking into the merciful eyes of Jesus he found hope. The last words that Therese wrote prior to her death sum up her teaching:

> I know for certain that even if I had on my conscience all the sins that can be committed I would go and cast myself in the arms of Jesus with a heart torn by repentance, for I know how much he cherishes the prodigal child that returns to him...[174]

Practical Love

Therese had an intense desire and longing to give her whole life to the Lord in love. She felt called to be a warrior, a priest, an apostle, a doctor, a martyr; to carry out the most heroic deeds for Jesus, her Beloved. She was happy to die for the Lord on some obscure foreign battlefield. To shed the last drop of her blood for him would be such a privilege. But all of this seemed to be so unreal because she was enclosed within a Carmelite monastery, not able to put a foot out in the world beyond the walls of the convent. Yet she knew the desires were in some way inspired by the Lord. What did it mean? Opening the Epistles of St Paul she came across the passage which proclaims "all cannot be apostles, prophets, doctors etc., that the Church is composed of different members, and that the eye cannot be the hand at one and the same time." Yet this did not give her peace. Then reading further, she found the sentence that brought consolation: "Yet strive after the better gifts, and I point out to you a yet more excellent way" (1Cor112:31). This more excellent way is love, and this is the way that leads most surely to God.

Therese could now see that while she did not recognise herself in any of the ministries described by Paul, or maybe she saw herself in all of them, it was love that gave her the key to her vocation. If the Church has a body with different members it must have a heart, and that heart was burning with love. It was love alone which made the Church's members act. The apostles would not preach the gospel without love; the martyrs would not shed their blood without love. "I understood that LOVE comprised all the vocations, that Love was everything, that it embraced all times and places…in a word it was eternal…at last I have found it…MY VOCATION IS LOVE."[175]

No one had ever read this text in this way before and it filled her with great serenity and purpose. But the love she was talking about was not just some passing affection. It was the love which Jesus showed us when he sacrificed himself on the Cross for us. Therese was very honest about her struggle to love. The relationships in her convent were intense and there was no escape from those whom she found difficult. It was for her a school of love and she candidly let us know how the Lord taught her. She knew that the command of Jesus, "Love one another as I have loved you", was not empty words. It had to be lived. Yet she knew it was impossible for her to love her sisters in this way, particularly those who annoyed her. Crying out to the Lord for help she realised that as long as she abided in Christ and he in her she could love, because he loved in and through her. She could love others because of Christ dwelling in her and empowering her. When she was charitable it was not really her work, but that of Christ within her. The virtue of practical love is given by God; it is not attained by our own strength or insight. Speaking to Jesus, she is delighted and grateful "that your will is to love in me all those you command me to love".[176] Again this is a dimension of her "little way"; realising her utter helplessness, weakness and impossibility, she relies fully on Jesus loving in her and through her.

Therese gives us some examples of loving when we have a natural aversion for someone. There was a sister who she found totally disagreeable in everything. She had a "natural antipathy" towards this woman. Not wanting to give into this negativity she decided to disregard the feelings and to love her by doing acts of kindness. She forced herself to do this over a long period of time. Great was her sense of victory when one day this sister asked her, "Would you tell me what attracts you so much towards me; every time you look at me, I see you smile?" Therese comments, "Ah what attracted me was Jesus hidden in the depths of her soul; Jesus who makes sweet what is bitter".[177]

Another example of practical love was when Therese volunteered to help Sr Pierre, who was quite feeble and a very grumpy soul, to make her way from the chapel to the refectory.[178] Therese found it impossible to please this cranky invalid. If she tried to be careful, she would be told she is going too fast; if she slowed down the poor lady would get impatient. And so it went on day after day. Therese found herself grow in love as she smiled radiantly at the troubled sister and helped her with her food. Overcoming her feelings of revulsion and humiliation she found love. It was a good example of the saying of John of the Cross, who Therese admired so much, "Where there is no love, put love, and you will find love".

THE HEART OF THE SAINTS

The Light of God's Love

The saints radiate the light of God's love in the world. They show us how to be holy. Far from trying to make sanctity happen by their own efforts, they were overtaken by the unmerited love of God as gift from on high and surrendered to his love with all their heart. Each of the stories related here speaks of weak men and women being persuaded by a tremendous divine Lover who is relentless in his pursuit of us, seeking to claim us as his own and win our unconditional love for him. Our God is a consuming fire. He totally respects our free will, but if we allow him entry into our hearts he ignites a fire of love within us that is unquenchable. No matter what vicissitudes we have to face in life, no matter what opposition we encounter in ministry, this quiet burning fire within sustains us and impels us forward in the calling he has made on our lives.

This fire is stoked in a particular way by meditation upon the passion of Jesus. The burning fire of love in the heart of Jesus as he died on the Cross moved the saints deeply, compelling them towards a passionate love in return. The madness of divine love in Jesus crucified captured their hearts. They felt overwhelmed by this sacrifice, awakening in them a love that knows no bounds, a love which expands the heart to embrace the world. Even the most mystical of these holy men and women were not simply caught up in a devotional vortex unconcerned for the plight of others. Their immersion into the mystery of Jesus crucified drew them into solidarity with the suffering of all men and women. Sharing the heart of Jesus for the lost, and for those most alienated, oppressed and abandoned, they gave themselves in intercession for others, in practical service of the poor and marginalised, and the proclamation of the good news of God's love to all men and women.

The Fire of the Spirit

Each of these saints was obviously filled with the Holy Spirit. But in keeping with the theology and spirituality of their time, they were relatively silent in their writings about the activity of the Holy Spirit. With their theology of redemption being so focussed on the suffering and death of Jesus, they do not show the same awareness of the saving significance of his resurrection. They all come from the Western spiritual tradition which until the twentieth century focussed heavily upon Good Friday, and much less on Easter Sunday. Consequently, while the experience of Pentecost is not overlooked, it is minimal in comparison to what we would want to express. All of these saints were conscious of Jesus' words, "I have come to bring fire to the earth and how I wish it were blazing already" (Lk 12:49), but they tended to speak of this only as the fire of love which burnt in his heart and was expressed most powerfully in his passion and death on the Cross. Certainly this perspective is immensely valuable. It is what in the first place has drawn me to them, because it resonates deeply within me. However, it is incomplete without a proclamation of the saving power of the Risen Christ and the outpouring of the fire of the Holy Spirit.

We need to complement the spiritual theology of these wonderful saints with an awareness of how Jesus was anointed with the Holy Spirit in his baptism in the Jordan, and how his ministry of preaching, healing and deliverance was exercised by the power of this messianic anointing. The fire he longed to bring to the earth was the fire of the Holy Spirit which was already burning within him, but could not be poured out on all flesh until his death and resurrection. Then at Pentecost, as Jesus promised, a ball of fire descended upon the apostles and others, with Mary in their midst, and then separated into tongues of fire over each one of them and "they were all filled with the Holy Spirit and began to speak in strange languages".

This Pentecostal fire of the Spirit moved the saints down through the ages to passionate love of God, zealous preaching and extraordinary works of mercy. As they gazed upon Jesus crucified, the Holy Spirit pierced their minds with the truth of who Jesus is as our Saviour and what he has done for us. The Holy Spirit, already given to them at baptism and confirmation, was released in power within them through their conversion experiences and this new fire of God's love made them irrepressible in a radical way of discipleship. They submitted to the sanctifying work of the Holy Spirit, cooperating with his transforming power, becoming the new creation God intended them to be. The Spirit within them made them bold in proclaiming the Good News; with such courage that, even if it meant the loss of their lives, they would rejoice in being given the privilege of suffering with Jesus. All of this and much more is implicit in their lives, but in our age when we are experiencing a "new Pentecost" in the Church we need to make this perspective of the powerful activity of the Holy Spirit in our sanctification and mission more explicit.

All are Called to be Saints

I can still hear within my heart the call of Pope John Paul II before World Youth Day 2000 challenging the young people not to be afraid to become "saints of the new millennium":

> You will ask me: but is it possible to be saints? If we had to rely only on human strength, the undertaking would be truly impossible... you are aware of the heavy burdens weighing on humanity, the many dangers which threaten us and the consequences caused by sins. At times we may be gripped by discouragement and even

come to think that it is impossible to change anything either in the world or in ourselves. Although the journey is difficult, we can do everything in the One who is our Redeemer. Turn then to no one but Jesus. Do not look elsewhere for what only he can give you, because 'of all the names in the world given to men this is the only one by which we can be saved' (Acts 4:12). With Christ, saintliness – the divine plan for every baptised person– becomes possible. Rely on him; believe in the invincible power of the Gospel and place faith as the foundation of your hope. Jesus walks with you, he renews your heart and strengthens you with the vigour of the Spirit.[179]

In his last message to young people before he died John Paul II made a similar heartfelt appeal: "The Church needs saints. All are called to holiness, and holy people alone can renew humanity".[180]

Responding to the Call

We see the saints of old making courageous choices, truly heroic decisions in following Jesus. Having heard his invitation they responded decisively and with great determination; a generous "yes" to the Lord and readiness to share with him in his Cross by a life of self-giving love. Having discovered the treasure of the love of God they knew the only way to respond was to give all to him, to surrender their lives without reservation. Instead of writing the script for their own life they now allowed the Lord to move in their lives according to his plan, rejoicing in his will as it unfolded in many unexpected but wonderful ways. Pope Francis told the young people at World Youth Day, Rio de Janeiro:

> God calls you to make definitive choices, and he has a plan for each of you: to discover that plan and to respond to your vocation is to move toward personal fulfilment. God calls each of us to be holy, to live his life, but he has a particular path for each one of us.[181]

Pope Francis challenged the young people to be revolutionaries and to "swim against the tide" of the current culture which sees everything as temporary; a culture "that ultimately believes you are incapable of responsibility, that believes you are incapable of true love". He called them not to be afraid to make a permanent commitment of love in marriage, or in consecrated life or priesthood. When the love of God is experienced in our hearts he will call us to the path marked out for us. True happiness, the real joy of the gospel, will be found when we respond with sacrificial love to his call. Whatever state of life the Lord calls us to embrace it will be our way to become saints, and it will be our way to be witnesses of the Good News of Jesus.

Becoming Saints

God puts a desire in us for him, so that we are only fulfilled through union with him. In the saints we see how he awakens that desire in the heart and it becomes insatiable; they passionately long for union with him. Jesus becomes the joy of their lives; he is everything. A passionate love for the Lord becomes the consuming desire of their life. Prayer is not a chore, even though it may be dry and dark with little palpable experience or enlightenment. Prayer is necessary for the soul to breathe. It is the relationship that keeps us alive. It's the only consolation for the soul, since it is being with one's best friend, the Beloved. Prayer is knowing one's nothingness, being acutely aware of one's brokenness, but not alarmed by this reality; rather it is letting Jesus be with me in this state of disrepair. It is knowing his accepting gaze upon me at all times and resting in the knowledge of his merciful love.

We notice how the saints fell upon the word of God to nourish the soul. Often words leapt off the page of the Scriptures and spoke immediately to the heart, especially in times of distress or calamity.

Even though their prayer became more and more contemplative, they never abandoned the scriptural word. Nor did they abandon their love for Jesus in his humanity, as he is revealed in the gospels. We are to return again and again to linger long with Jesus in the gospel texts and allow him to form us according to his heart. A privileged place must be given to his passion and death on the Cross. Who cannot be moved to love by dwelling upon Jesus crucified? Here the fire of love is enflamed within us again by the Holy Spirit.

But our proclamation to the world is first and foremost "Jesus is Lord!" We preach Jesus crucified, but by this we mean the saving event of *both* his death *and* resurrection. He has been "raised up" first on the Cross for us, and then by the Father in glorious resurrection. He is now the Risen Lord, still bearing his wounds as signs of love for all. We were baptised into his death and resurrection; immersed into the transforming power of his resurrection. Joined with him in the tomb, the old self was put to death. Joined with him in glorious resurrection, we have the power to become a new creation. The Holy Spirit comes to apply to our lives this amazing new power of transformation. Resurrection power is given to us. The victory of Jesus over sin and death becomes our victory.

Only the Holy Spirit can make us holy. He is the great change agent in our lives. The saints simply surrendered to his action, allowing the transforming work of the Spirit to take place within them, by embracing prayer, self-denial, the Eucharist, and the sacrament of Reconciliation, and a life of service. Breaking the power of the flesh, overcoming the ingrained patterns of sin, forming in us a new mind, according to the mind of Christ – all is the work of the Spirit. As we are set free from our former enslavement, the Spirit makes us a new creation, bearing the fruits of love, joy, peace, patience, kindness, faithfulness, generosity, gentleness, and self-control.

God Calls the Weak

Becoming holy is to become like Jesus, to have his heart for others, and to love as he has loved. All this can seem impossible, and way beyond our capacity. That is the main point. By ourselves it *is* impossible. As Jesus said, "cut off from me you can do nothing" (Jn 15:6). Often hagiographers do us a disfavour by painting the saints as super heroes achieving marvellous miracles and exercising extraordinary human strength. While we ought not discount their heroic virtue and charismatic gifting, we need to touch into the reality of their lives and their human weaknesses. I find it helpful to notice that Ignatius Loyola was tempted to commit suicide, that Alphonsus Liguori suffered from scruples all his life right up to his death-bed, that Teresa of Avila occasionally became angry with God when things didn't turn out as she wanted, that Catherine of Siena was unfairly judgmental of her best friend and confidante, that Clare had to be restrained by Francis from trying too hard to be a saint, and so on. The only people God has to work with are weak human beings who struggle desperately to follow him and often mess it up badly. He is rich in mercy. I have no doubt that is why Francis de Sales was so intent upon teaching us to be gentle with ourselves; because he himself as a young man had succumbed to some degree to the Calvinist image of a harsh, unrelenting, punitive God.

The road to sainthood, as Therese of Lisieux has shown, is not by rigorously trying to drag ourselves up the ladder of holiness only to fall off in miserable failure again and again. Yes, we aim towards virtue, but we know it is all God's work. Making friends with our brokenness, and being at home with our neediness, is fundamental. This is what draws the Lord to us. He did not come for those who are well, but for the sick; he did not come for the virtuous, but for sinners. The Lord loves to exalt the lowly. So as long as we don't fall into discouragement and self-pity it is good to be in touch with the desperate state of our human condition. The words spoken to Paul are forever relevant, "My grace is enough for you, my power is at its best in weakness".

Missionary Disciples

The saints were missionaries of God's love. That is our calling also. The Spirit of love has been given to us in baptism. At Confirmation we were anointed with the same Spirit of Jesus for mission. Evangelisation is not just for the "professionals", it is rather the joyful task of all in the Church. Pope Francis reminds us that "in virtue of their baptism all members of the Church have become missionary disciples".[182] We are by definition missionaries of God's love. The Pope insists, "Anyone who has truly experienced God's saving love does not need much time or lengthy training to go out and proclaim that love". Once we know the joy of the Risen Christ, having met him personally, and welcomed him into our hearts, we cannot contain our love for him, and it must overflow in sharing the Good News of God's saving love with others.

We have seen how Francis of Assisi was so filled with joy in the Lord that he had to go forth to bring this love to others. When he heard the words of the gospel about Jesus sending out the seventy two disciples he responded, "This is what I must do!" So for ourselves. The call of Jesus to "go make disciples" is upon us in the same way. When Dominic encountered the inn keeper who was hopelessly confused by the Cathari heresy, he spoke the truth in love with such clarity that the man's mind and heart was changed. So also for ourselves. In a world of so many competing philosophies and ways of life we have the opportunity, indeed the duty, to proclaim the truth that will set people free, guiding them to Jesus who is the truth, the way and the life. When Ignatius Loyola was in a cave at

Manresa he realised deep within his spirit why he was on this earth – to give glory to God and to work for the salvation of all men and women. That was his life; and it is ours as well.

Whichever way the Lord calls us in life we are meant to be missionaries of his saving love. He will show us the way. When Francis de Sales set out to convert the people in the Chablais region he was armed with nothing but the gentleness of the heart of Jesus and openness to speak the words which Jesus would give him to speak. The results were remarkable. So also for us. We live in a different context with diverse challenges, but the same Holy Spirit is inspiring us to go forth with the fire of God's love to proclaim boldly the joy that every human heart needs. When Alphonsus Liguori experienced those simple shepherds on the Amalfi coast who were so hungry for God's word he did not hesitate to respond. He threw himself vigorously into missionary work for the most abandoned. This is our challenge as well. All around us people are living distressed and anxious lives without meaning and purpose, weighed down by life's burdens with nowhere to find relief, and no one to show them the way to true peace. This is our calling; this is who we are.

Endnotes

1. *Legend of the Three Companions* 2:6.
2. Ibid., 3:7.
3. Ibid., 5:13.
4. Ibid., 6:20.
5. *The Testament of Francis*, in *Writings and Early Biographies*, (Chicago: Franciscan Herald Press, 1972) p. 67.
6. Little Flowers, 25.
7. Thomas of Celano, *First Life*, 30: 84-85.
8. *Letter to All Friars*, *Writings and Early Biographies*, p. 106.
9. *The Testament*, op. cit., p. 68.
10. Little Flowers 16.
11. *Anonymous Perugian*, 3:16.
12. Earlier Rule 5 (c.f. Admonitions 25).
13. *Admonitions*, 8.
14. Ibid., 18.
15. Ibid., 9.
16. Ibid., 11.
17. *Earlier Rule*, 10.
18. *Admonitions* 25.
19. *Earlier Rule* 5.
20. Ibid., 4.
21. Little Flowers 26 in *Writings and Biographies*, p. 1360.
22. Ibid., 16.
23. Ibid., 21.
24. Thomas of Celano, *Life of Francis*, 1,29,81
25. Pope Francis, *Laudato Si*, 10-12.
26. *Little Flowers,* 1-4.

27 Ibid., 8.
28 The Legend of St Clare 4 in *Clare of Assisi, Early Documents*, ed. Regis J Armstrong, (New York: Paulist Press,1988).
29 Ibid., 8.
30 Process of Canonisation 17:4 quoted in Marco Bartoli, *Clare of Assisi*, (London: Darton, Longman and Todd, 1993) p. 50.
31 This whole episode in *The Legend of St Clare*, 24-26.
32 This story in *Little Flowers* 15.
33 Thomas of Celano, *Second Legend*, CLV11, p. 207.
34 *Process* 7, 3.
35 *Little Flowers*, 35.
36 Thomas of Celano, *The Legend of St Clare*.
37 *Process* 11, 2.
38 *The Legend of Clare* 30.
39 The fourth Letter to Blessed Agnes, in Henri Daniel-Rops, *The Call of St Clare* (NY: Hawthorn, 1963) p. 131.
40 Ibid.
41 Clare of Assisi, *Early Documents*, 83.
42 Testament, p. 68.
43 Much of Dominic's early history can be gleaned from this source: Jordan of Saxony, *On the Beginnings of the Order*, trans by Simon Tugwell. Parable. U.S.A. 1982. I have followed also the account given by Guy Bedouelle OP, *Saint Dominic:The grace of the Word*, (San Francisco:Ignatius Press, 1987). For documents from early times see Early Dominicans, ed.Simon Tugwell OP (N.Y: Paulist Press, 1982).
44 Ibid., 34.
45 This term which is derived from the Latin, "mendicare" meaning to beg, was applied to both Francis and Dominic and others, who lived absolute poverty, relying on others to be the means of God's provision, being itinerant preachers of the gospel, while still living a community life of prayer and brotherhood.
46 Jordan of Saxony, *The Beginnings*, 47.
47 Sr Mary Jean Dorcy OP, *Saint Dominic*,(St Louis: Herder, 1987) p. 81-83.

[48] *Nine Ways of Prayer of Saint Dominic*, ed. and trans. by Simon Tugwell (Dublin: Dominican Publications, 1978) p. 15. This is the primary source for Dominic's way of prayer.

[49] Ibid., p. 38.

[50] Catherine of Siena, *The Dialogue*, p.158

[51] *The Dialogue*, p. 153.

[52] Prayer 11 in Mary Driscoll OP, *Catherine of Siena: selected spiritual writings* (NY: New City Press, 1993) p. 69.

[53] Raymond of Capua, *The Life of Catherine of Siena* 1:11. Much of what we know about Catherine's life was given in this book written by her friend and spiritual director who knew her closely. Further references will simply be to "Raymond".

[54] Raymond, 2.1 For a good treatment of the themes in Catherine's teaching, see Mary Ann Fatula OP, *Catherine of Siena's Way*, Collegeville, Minnesota: The Liturgical Press, 1987.

[55] Raymond 2.4.

[56] Raymond 2.6.

[57] *The Dialogue* 69.

[58] Ibid., 134.

[59] Ibid., 4

[60] Ibid., 8.

[61] Ibid.

[62] Prayer 19.

[63] Raymond 1.6.

[64] Ibid., 1.10.

[65] *The Dialogue*, 135.

[66] *Letter* 368.

[67] *Letter* 249.

[68] *Letter* 253.

[69] *The Dialogue* 128.

[70] Ibid., 75.

[71] *Letter* 163.

72. *The Dialogue*, 129.
73. *Letter*, 173.
74. *The Dialogue*, 66.
75. Ibid., 136.
76. Ibid., 144.
77. Ibid., 145.
78. Ibid., 124.
79. Raymond 1.10.
80. *The Dialogue* 119.
81. The early spiritual journey of Ignatius can be traced in his autobiography, *A Pilgrim's Journey*, Wilmington, Delaware: Michael Glazier, 1985. See also Karl Rahner, *Ignatius Loyola*, London: Collins, 1978.
82. Ibid., p. 30.
83. Ibid., p.38
84. Ibid., pp. 38-39.
85. Ibid., p 39.
86. Louis J Puhl, *The Spiritual Execises of St Ignatius*, (Chicago: St Paul, 1951) p. 22.
87. Ibid., p. 62.
88. Puhl., p. 119.
89. Ibid.
90. Puhl, p. 120.
91. Ibid., p. 124.
92. Ibid., p. 125.
93. Ibid., p. 70.
94. Ibid.
95. A useful summary of Ignatius' discernment can be found in Timothy Gallagher, *Discerning the Will of God*, New York: Crossroad Publishing, 2009
96. Letter written to Ignatius from Cochin in January 1154
97. Quoted in Office of Readings on Feast day of Francis Xavier
98. The stories of these martyrs are well documented in John O'Brien, *The First Martyrs of North America*, New York: All Saints Press, 1963.

99. Teresa of Avila, *The Book of her Life*, Collected Works of St Teresa of Avila, Vol I, (Washington DC, ICS publications, 1987) 8.7.
100. Ibid., 9.1,3.
101. Ibid., 9.8.
102. Ibid., 8.2.
103. Ibid., 8.5.
104. *The Way of Perfection*, 21.2 in Collected Works Vol II (Washingston DC: ICS publications, 1980).
105. Ibid., 25.3.
106. *The Book of Life*, 22.7.
107. *The Way of Perfection*, 28.4.
108. Ibid., 28.5.
109. *Interior Castle* IV.3,2 in Collected Works Vol II
110. Ibid., IV 1,7.
111. *The Way of Perfection*, 2.
112. Ibid., 31,7.
113. *Interior Castle*, IV 3,9.
114. Ibid., IV 10.
115. *The Way of Perfection* 31,8.
116. See *The Life*, 11.6 onwards.
117. See his Third Advent Homily 2016 at Zenit.org/articles/special-3rd-advent-sermon-from-fr-cantalamesssa.[118] For his life story one can read Andre Ravier SJ, *Francis de Sales: Sage and Saint* (San Francisco: Ignatius Press,1988).
119. *Introduction to the Devout Life*, NY: Random House, 2002.
120. Ibid., Part 1,1.
121. Fr Ken Barker, *Becoming Fire*, (Melbourne: Freedom publishing, 2001) p 1
122. *The Love of God* Book 2,5, trans., abridged by Vincent Kerns (India: SFS Publications).
123. Ibid., Book 2,8.
124. Ibid., Book 2.12.
125. Ibid., Book 2.12.

[126] Ibid., Book 2.13.
[127] Ibid., Book 2.21.
[128] Ibid., Book 5.1.
[129] Ibid., Book 5.2.
[130] Ibid., Book 5.3.
[131] Ibid., Book 4.4. Note translation uses the word "sympathy", but "empathy" is closer to what is meant
[132] Ibid., Book 5.4.
[133] Ibid., Book 5.5.
[134] Ibid., Book 8.2.
[135] Ibid., Book 5.4.
[136] Ibid., Book 9.10.
[137] Introduction 3.11.
[138] Ibid., 3.9.
[139] Ibid., 4.11.
[140] Ibid., 4.12.
[141] St Margaret Mary Alocoque, *The Autobiography*, trans. Vincent Kerns (London: Darton, Longman and Todd) p ix
[142] See Timothy T. O'O'donnell, STD, *Heart of the Redeemer*, (San Francisco: Ignatius Press, 1989)
[143] Pius XII, Haurietis Aquas, quoted in *Heart of the Redeemer*, p.78
[144] Adversus Haereses V,1,1
[145] Ibid., IV, 18,2.
[146] Enarrationes in 12 Psalmos 1,33.
[147] This movement which had its beginnings with Gerard Groote (1340-1384) had a strong influence on Thomas a Kempis, the author of the *Imitation of Christ*.
[148] Thomas a Kempis, Prayers and Meditations on the Life of Christ, quoted by Timothy O'Donnelly, *Heart of the Redeemer*, p. 113.
[149] Francis de Sales, The Love of God, 5.12.
[150] St Margaret Mary Alocoque, *The Autobiography*, pp. 44-45.
[151] Ibid.

[152] Ibid pp., 46-47.
[153] Ibid., pp., 48-49.
[154] For an authoritative biography see Frederick M. Jones, *Alphonsus de Liguori*, Dublin: Gill and McMillan, 1992. See also Sister Nancy Fearon IHM, *Never Stop Walking: The Life and Spirit of St Alphonsus Liguori*, Michigan: Sisters Servants of the Immaculate Heart of Mary, 1977.
[155] The most accessible source for this perspective is Alphonsus Liguori, *The Love of God in Practice*.
[156] These ways of obtaining love are to be found in *The Love of God in Practice*, op.cit., passim.
[157] Alphonsus Liguori, *The Prayer of Petition*, Ballarat: Majellan Press, 1965.
[158] Frederick M. Jones, op.cit., p. 260.
[159] Frederick M. Jones, *Alphonsus de Liguori*, p. 253.
[160] *The Story of a Soul* (Washington DC: ICS Publications, 1976) p. 77.
[161] Ibid., p. 98.
[162] Ibid., p. 99.
[163] Ibid., p. 207.
[164] Ibid.
[165] Ibid.
[166] *Her Last Conversations* (Washington, DC:ICS Publications,1977) pp. 138-9.
[167] Ibid., p. 129.
[168] Francois Jamart O.C.D. *Complete Spiritual Doctrine of Therese of Liseux*, (N.Y: Alba House, 1961) p. 64.
[169] Letters of Therese of Lisieux, 191.
[170] Frome the process of beatification, quoted by Aloysius Rego, *Holiness for All: Themes from St Therese of Liseux*, Oxford: Teresian Press, 2009. This little primer on Therese is excellent.
[171] *Story of a Soul*, p. 180.
[172] Ibid., pp. 180-81.
[173] Patrick Ahern, *Maurice and Therese: The Story of Love*, London: Darton, Longman and Todd, 1998.
[174] *Story of a Soul*, p. 259.

175 Ibid., p. 194.
176 Ibid., p. 221.
177 Ibid., p. 223.
178 Ibid., pp. 247-248.
179 Message of the Holy Father to the Youth of the World on the Occasion of the 15th World Youth Day, 3, Vatican, June 29th 1999, Solemnity of Saints Peter and Paul.
180 Message of the Holy Father to the Youth of the World on the occasion of the 20th World Youth Day (Cologne, August 2005), 7, given at Castel Gandolfo, 6 August 2004.
181 Address of Pope Francis, Meeting with the Volunteers of the 28th World Youth Day, Rio de Janeiro, 28th July 2013
182 Pope Francis, *Evangelii Gaudium*, 120.

www.ingramcontent.com/pod-product-compliance
Lightning Source LLC
Chambersburg PA
CBHW070549160426
43199CB00014B/2432